The Dance
of Person and Place

SUNY series in Living Indigenous Philosophies

Agnes B. Curry and Anne Waters, editors

The Dance of Person and Place

One Interpretation of American Indian Philosophy

Thomas M. Norton-Smith

Published by State University of New York Press, Albany

For information, contact State University of New York Press, Albany, NY
www.sunypress.edu

Production by Ryan Morris
Marketing by Anne M. Valentine

Library of Congress Cataloging-in-Publication Data

Norton-Smith, Thomas M., 1954-
 The dance of person and place : one interpretation of American Indian
philosophy / Thomas M. Norton-Smith.
       p. cm. — (SUNY series in living indigenous philosophies)
   Includes bibliographical references and index.
   ISBN 978-1-4384-3133-8 (hardcover : alk. paper)
   ISBN 978-1-4384-3132-1 (pbk. : alk. paper)
   1. Indian philosophy—North America. I. Title.

   E98.P5N67 2010
   970.004'97—dc22   2009033704

                    10 9 8 7 6 5 4 3 2 1

Each nation of Indians was made by the Great Spirit, in the skies, and when they were finished He brought them down and gave them a place upon the Earth. To the Shawnees he was more favorable than to any others. He gave them a piece of His own heart.

—Black Hoof (Trowbridge in Kinietz and Voegelin 1939: 61)

Contents

Illustrations

Foreword

May we add more beauty to the world . . .

We come to a place in the history of the First Nations of the Americas wherein a confluence of intellectual and political movements affecting academe has brought some of our indigenous students, faculty, and local knowledge bearers to the forefront of gate keeping. On one hand, more than ever before, members of our indigenous communities are entering academic professions and assuming positions whereby we can speak for ourselves. On the other, our ever precious local indigenous knowledge, as it spans throughout the world, has come to the attention of those who would seek to use and thereby profit from it. Laurie Whitt, among other scholars, has for many years addressed this commodification and expropriation of global indigenous knowledge.

This series is begun at a time when the global economy crumbles before the eyes of the world. It comes at a time when eyes focus upon the future of our planet in all the wonderment of our situatedness within larger galaxies. It comes at a time when alternative ways of being in the world are announcing their presence. Solar panels and wind turbines are dotting the landscapes of Western Europe and the United States. The love affair with gasoline engines and super fast cars is coming to a close, as people reach for a better way to use planetary resources. Some are even questioning whether thinking of the earth's gifts as "resources" is appropriate. Most automobile engines are now made in Japan, and China now leads the world in manufacturing new technologies of everything from solar panels to LED lights.

Indigenous communities occupy sensitive and contradictory positions in this global landscape. Often at the forefront of risk, with our ways of being literally demolished, our communities also respond with strong undertones of resilience and adaptability. In spite of centuries of genocidal aggression, indigenous ways of thinking have not been destroyed but rather transmuted. New technologies enter our indigenous communities at this same time that a tremendous economic upheaval is occurring. This upheaval is due to the ambitious greed of gangs that seek to extract billions and trillions of dollars through large global corporations without so much as a hint of responsibility. It is perhaps time to ask a few questions and seek some input from our traditional indigenous philosophers, and in so doing, once again ask some of those centuries old on-going questions that philosophers are known to ponder.

Some may ask, "Why philosophers?" Are there any traditional indigenous philosophers? And how could western oriented and indigenous scholars even begin to meet on a horizon to communicate across diverse cultural variances of time and space?

Vine Deloria reminds us that academic philosophers have long been held out as those who hold keys to the gates of philosophy, the "capstone discipline" of the western academy. And the western academy has, for a long time, yielded access to only a biased history of the development of intellectual thought. Yet to the extent that there has been any dialogue among western philosophers with traditional indigenous philosophers, it has been only after long travels, in quiet corners with patient questions, and contemplative responses found in the backloads of our global countryside.

Traditional indigenous scholars, and living indigenous philosophies, come in small doses to the western academic world. Such ideas, whether about pharmaceutical herbs, emotional healing ceremony, or communal ways of being, have been shared thus far only in small circles. These circles have begun to expand, as Gregory Cajete tells us, since our students have taken up the task of drawing together, for example, western and indigenous science. Circles of knowledge sharing among indigenous scholars however, have generally not been accessible to academe, much less the general population. And perhaps the time has come to change this, and make some efforts to share those things that individual indigenous communities would like to share with others.

The question why particular indigenous groups might want to share information about various ways of being, living, and acting in consonance with the world we inhabit has many answers, perhaps as diverse as the numbers of communities that exist. But one clear answer is that there may be a need to move toward a global culture in order for humans to survive. This does not preclude the continuance and development or retention of some of our traditional knowings or ways of being. Rather it is merely a recognition that it may take some cumulative knowledge of humanity brought together in order for us to survive the difficult governmental and resource problems that face the world today.

To the extent that our traditional indigenous scholars have long been informing the more recent settlers and their intellectual spokespersons that there is a circularity of life, and that everything is interconnected for a reason, so also have we been naming the possibilities of expanding our knowledge bases. Indigenous scholars have always traveled from place to place to return to their origin. Ted Jojola has brought this to our attention, and Thomas Norton-Smith, in this volume, returns us to that thought. It is then in this context that Native Americans—Indians—of the Americas can ask questions such as, "How do Indians fit into the contemporary engagement of enlightenment scholarship as it struggles to come to terms with earthly realities of global warming and biological warfare?" or "Why might it be important to have dialogue between the cognitively 'academically programmed' and 'indigenously programmed' philosophers?" In asking these questions, others equally important come to mind as a preamble to discussion. And some of these questions are addressed in this text.

Some of the questions raised in this text are significant because they query the grounds of our abilities to understand one another. Thomas asks, for instance, "What classifications or categories of ontology can be used to cross over divergent philosophies?" In an effort to come to terms with the cacophony of voices across the many cultures, both indigenous and modern, he wants to know whether there are culturally relative ontologies that inform our ability to cognize differently. And Thomas also raises meta-ethical questions in the context of diverse cultures: "What, if anything, does it mean to engage in talk about 'right action' or a 'good red road'?"; or "Is there any meta-ethics that can guide human principles of action, or that might suggest a commonality of reasoned moral action?" And while some might ask if raising these questions can speak to our current problems of limited resources and overpopulation, others might ask whether humans can afford not to raise these questions considering our precarious positioning in the universe.

We enter into a new age of intellectual enlightenment by bringing into play different ideas about what it means to be human, and to what extent humans are of necessity communal beings. Contemporary inferences of our responses to these all important questions that all cultures contemplate may make the difference between, as we say in Indian Country, "getting it right or not." And in the context of getting it right, this may mean survival of our species on this planet. In our scholarship to "get it right," it is important to ask about indigenous and western intellectual commonalities, and consider what differences of significance might they offer, that can speak to our current globalization of the academic voice.

As a dear friend of mine is prone to remind me, "How can we dialogue about 'wombats' if you don't know what a wombat is, have never seen

*It is time to globalize the academic voice.

one, and don't know how it acts in the world?" To this I respond, "That is the old 'gavagai' problem of W. V. O. Quine" or "That is the problem of constructed world views."—which is only to say that we don't know how to get rid of biological warfare if we don't know what it is. And we will never understand our neighbors if we cannot come to meaningful communication about what is in the world and how we, as humans, might have a role to play in the world, and how that may be done.

This series is neither about, as western philosophers might say, whether "Wittgensteinians" understand language, nor about whether "Goodmanians" can construct a better world, nor even whether "Habermasians" can communicate. It is rather, about making some effort to scribe some information that has been cast aside by a large portion of those who dominate the politico of human knowledge. It is about a hope that documenting some thoughts and ideas about the ways worlds are, and how humans live in those worlds, might enable us to realize the vastness from which our ideas are born, and the immeasurable openness to which we may turn for creativity. It is about opening the life of our voices to the immense task that lies before us, as human, and as beings in the world, to reach for the horizon of our new worlds. In this spirit, we reach to overcome the dogma of ways and beliefs that no longer work, to return in wonder at the ways and beliefs that have worked in the past, and perhaps to recreate, from the ashes of the commodified halls of western knowledge, a new resurgence of that which is what means, in a positive way, to be human.

The origin of this series is to permit voice for our indigenous philosophies that continue to live, and that have allowed humans to live, in community with our surrounding environment. The consequences of bringing forth voices of living indigenous philosophies for contemplation by ones who would bravely philosophize about them, have yet to be known. Whether themes of cosmological shifts, themes of kinship relations among animated beings, or themes of transformative powers in worlds that open to us, we are all in this together. And this is what Thomas reminds us of in his work. It matters not whether you are of Hopewell descent or Anasazi condominiums, of desert or wind or water or forest or mountain culture—we are all in this together, and in this we are bound, as tightly as the butterfly in a cocoon.

Anne Waters and Agnes Curry
20 March 2009

Acknowledgments

There are many who contributed to this work in innumerable ways—so many, in fact, that I will surely forget someone, and for that I apologize. I thank series editors Agnes Curry and Anne Waters for their comments and encouragement. I owe much to Piqua Sept Shawnee tribal elders Jim Perry (who recently passed), Don Rankin, and Rick Wagar. As well, I have benefited from counsels with clan and tribal members Bryan Dabe, Duane Everhart (even though he's a Turtle), and Bob and Helen Griffin. Kent State University colleagues John Harkness, Leslie Heaphy, Bradley Keefer, and Mel May reviewed various iterations of the manuscript—and we're still friends! Roger Davis chased down the Squier and Davis map of the Newark Works—what would we do without librarians? Sharon Schreffler helped in *every* way in preparing the manuscript—what would we do without faculty secretaries? Students Steven Gandee, Kris Kurian, Michael Lemon, and Car-li Waller helped crystallize many thoughts developed herein while enrolled in a section of *American Indian Philosophy* at Kent State Stark Campus. Kris Kurian made some critical contributions to the text, and she helped format the bibliography as well. (And all I had to do in return was to haul her bookcase in my truck!) This work could not have been completed without a Faculty Professional Improvement Leave from Kent State University and funding for an undergraduate research assistant from the Kent State Stark Campus. Perhaps the most valued and valuable input and influence came from Michael Byron, Agnes Curry, Lee Hester, Lorraine Mayer, and Kyle Whyte, who participated in a panel discussion of the manuscript—which aptly bore the working title "The Burden"—at the 2009 American Philosophical Association Central Division meetings in Chicago; however, we very much missed Scott Pratt and Sandra Tomsons.

I also owe thanks to the unnamed copy editors at SUNY Press (who hate the words "while" and "upon," by the way) who turned my clunky prose into something even more than presentable.

I would like to thank Beverly Slavin for her kind permission to reprint "Two Plus Two or Why Indians Flunk." *Through Indian Eyes: The Native*

Experience in Books for Children. Eds. Beverly Slapin and Doris Seale. Berkeley: Oyate Publishers, 2006.

Finally, I owe many thanks and much love to my ever supportive companions: Abby Wallace, my eastern gray squirrel person; Max, our Siamese cat person (who is trying to help me type at this very moment—but he has no thumbs); and especially my 25 year love, Linda Lee—who just happens to be my *human* person.

I

Common Themes in American Indian Philosophy

This chapter introduces the four common themes that are the focus of the interpretation of American Indian philosophy as *a dance of person and place*: relatedness and circularity as world-ordering principles, the expansive conception of persons, and the semantic potency of performance. It also offers a few clarifications and caveats that must frame the discussion, and explains why crafting a *rational reconstruction* of the "traditional" American Indian world version might be our best and only hope. Finally, it introduces the somewhat remarkable notion that *an American Indian world version constructs a well-made, actual world* from a culturally sophisticated constructivist perspective grounded in the philosophy of Nelson Goodman.

First Introductions

kiwaakomelepwa! nitesiθo miyaaθwe natoke. saawanwa nilla no'ki ni m'soma peleawa.[1] Greetings to you all! My name is Owl Listening. I am Shawnee and my clan is Turkey. The elder who dreamed my name, Michael Spivey, passed recently, and this work remembers him.

I present one possible interpretation of American Indian philosophy as *a dance of person and place* by examining four important notions—common themes, if you will—that seem to recur across American Indian traditions: two world-ordering principles, relatedness and circularity, the expansive conception of persons, and the semantic potency of performance. My exploration views Native philosophy through the lens of a culturally sophisticated constructivism grounded in the work of analytic philosopher Nelson Goodman.[2] This work, then, also remembers Jim Parmenter, the elder, colleague, and friend who first introduced me to the philosophy of Professor Goodman.

I need to say something at the outset about the Western philosophical tradition—the tradition of Plato and Aristotle, Descartes and Hume, Quine and Goodman—and my place in it. The Western intellectual tradition deserves a close political analysis from a Native standpoint, and contemporary American Indian critics are now beginning to take on that task.[3] Indeed, I won't be able to resist the occasional historical or political observation, pointing out Western prejudices or biases, in the reflections to come. My purpose, however, is not to critique the Western tradition, but to argue that—contrary to centuries of condescension and derision—an American Indian world version makes a legitimate world, *even within a culturally sophisticated Western constructivist framework.*

As for my own history and bias, I am mixed-blood Shawnee and an enrolled member of the Piqua Sept Shawnee Tribe; but I am also well schooled in the concepts and methodologies of Western philosophy of mathematics and logic. I am not undertaking this project because I have some special expertise or clarity about issues in contemporary philosophy—the debate between realism and constructivism among them. Nor have I some special insight into and about Native world versions; I am neither an elder nor one with medicine. In fact, I know of others who have that special knowledge, expertise, and insight into each of these traditions. I am undertaking this interpretation of American Indian philosophy because I happen to be at a special place and time, where and when American Indian philosophy is on the verge of legitimacy within the discipline of philosophy; perhaps my efforts may be an "Open Door" for the Native philosophers who can do the better job. I speak for no one but myself, so any errors are mine alone; and there will be errors, for my understanding of the traditional American Indian worldview is evolving, perhaps as yours is. Know well that I will say nothing that a diligent scholar couldn't find somewhere in print, for the rest belongs to the People, and it is not my place to share it.

Before beginning my promised constructivist interpretation of American Indian philosophy, I must offer a few clarifications and caveats, some of which may be a bit sobering. The first is deceptively nontrivial: What is the appropriate way to refer to the indigenous people called *Indians?* Of course, it is currently trendy, especially within the academy, to use "Native American," but I reject the label—perhaps shockingly—in favor of "American Indian," despite the fact that "Indian" is a name imposed by colonial powers that recalls the disease, depredations, and dispossessions Native peoples have suffered at their hands. However, I know of no Indian who really appreciates being called a "Native American."

First, the name "Native American," fashioned after "African American" and similar labels, suggests that Indians are American citizens who just happen to be of Native descent. However, unlike African or Asian Americans, who *are* American citizens of African or Asian descent, Indians are also proud citizens of *sovereign* Indian nations—Cherokee, Choctaw, and Shawnee among them—so the "politically" appropriate label misconstrues and inaccurately portrays the actual political situation. Unlike her Asian American neighbor, who is an American and state citizen, an enrolled Cherokee woman is a citizen of a third sovereign entity: The Cherokee Nation.

I once heard an Indian voicing a second perhaps more compelling reason for rejecting the label "Native American."[4] He argued that the approximately 390 treaties struck between the federal government and various tribes refer to indigenous nations by name or to "Indians." In fact, Article 1, Section 8 of the U.S. Constitution empowers the Congress "[t]o regulate Commerce with foreign Nations, and among the several States, and with the Indian Tribes" (Mount 2007). "If we begin calling ourselves 'Native Americans' and not 'Indians,'" he argued, "then that will just give the federal government another way to abrogate the old treaties, because the treaties were made with Indians, but all of the Indians will be gone—*replaced by Native Americans.*"

Anyway, Indians call themselves "Indians," both formally and informally, as the National Congress of American Indians and the American Indian Philosophical Association illustrate. So, rather than adopt some monstrous invention like "Amerindian," or some overbroad and imprecise labels like "indigenous" or "aboriginal people," I'll stick with "American Indians" (and sometimes "Indians" or "Natives"). This usage has the additional virtue that folks who *are* Indian will know that I'm talking about them.

I offer yet a second clarification before my investigation begins. Just as in the case of Western philosophy, there is no monolithic set of beliefs that constitute *the* American Indian philosophy. At the time of first contact with Europeans, there were hundreds of Native tribes and nations, each with its own culture, language, history, origin story, and ceremonial cycle—even with its own "intellectualism," or ways of thinking about the world:

> Philosophical differences between American Indian intellectualism and mainstream intellectualism are actually based on the differences among the various tribal cultures. Hence, the difference is not accurately between "Indian intellectualism and mainstream intellectualism" but between mainstream intellectualism and *the different tribes' intellectualism.* (Fixico 2003: 13, emphasis added)

That said, there are a number of notions or ways of regarding the world—I call them *themes*—that seem to recur across various American Indian traditions. The four I consider—relatedness and circularity as world-ordering principles, the expansive conception of persons, and the semantic potency of performance—together comprise one possible interpretation of Indian philosophy. Another interpreter might identify and develop a different set of common themes.

A third clarification must preface this constructivist interpretation of Native philosophy. In Western thought we draw easy distinctions between various branches of knowledge—religions and sciences, technologies and humanities among them. If evidence for the claim is necessary, simply consider how Western universities are organized into isolated departments tucked within college "silos"; although there are obvious connections, no one confuses philosophy and science, religion and history, or music and literature. However, there are no such easy distinctions between various realms of knowledge in American Indian traditions, as Brian Burkhart (2004) observes:

> Literature and philosophy, science and religion are all very different branches of knowledge in Western thought. Out of these four, most consider only two, science and philosophy, to be branches of knowledge at all. The other two are thought to be entirely different ways in which humans express their being in the world. However, in American Indian thought this is not the case. None of these four can really be separated from the others. (22)

The consequence is that there is no analogue of Western philosophy—understood as an isolated and self-contained discipline posing a set of fundamental questions about reality, knowledge, and value, and attempting to answer those questions with some sort of rational methodology—in American Indian world versions. That said, ontological, epistemological, and axiological beliefs and actions abound in Native world versions, and so in that sense there are beliefs and actions that we may confidently designate "philosophical."

Nicholas Black Elk's narrative, shared with John Neihardt, provides a perfect example of the seamlessness of Native knowledge. First published in 1932, *Black Elk Speaks* is at once a religious and moral text, a personal and tribal history, poetry, medicine, song, and dance. Described by Vine Deloria as a standard by which any newly emerging "great religious classic" must be judged, the poignant Black Elk narrative is the account of a Lakota holy man who, given a powerful vision early in life, is unable to harness fully the power of the vision in the service of his people. At one point in the narrative, Black Elk's (2000) description of a "happy summer" of hunting, fishing, and cutting tepee poles flows seamlessly into a moral story, "High Horse's Courting," which teaches how one should and should not conduct oneself in order to "get a girl when you wanted to be married"

(47–58). At another point, a historical account of the Lakota's sorrows at being removed to a reservation moves through a detailed description of a lamenting ceremony and the resulting religious vision (136–44). I note, of course, that my description here erects the kinds of artificial boundaries that are really absent in American Indian knowledge.

I often use *Black Elk Speaks* and similar narratives, told or written by Indians, but interpreted or edited by Western writers, cultural anthropologists, and ethnographers as examples or evidence, but this immediately presents a pair of very sobering challenges to my project. The first challenge is determining when a source is reliable, that is, when a work conveys an unvarnished and untarnished Native world version, and when, on the other hand, a source is suspect. You see, American Indian traditions are oral traditions wherein tribal culture, knowledge, history, and values—all of the elements of a Native world version—are transmitted from elder to youth through story. However, until quite recently the American Indian world version has suffered from the Western sociological dogma that culture evolves from the primitive to the civilized, much as a species evolves. "And, given that Western culture is the *most* civilized," goes the dogma, "every world version that is *different* must be more primitive, hence inferior, since 'primitive' means 'inferior.'" In his comments about the "native races of North America," ethnographer J. W. Powell (1877) observes that:

> The opinions of a savage people are childish. Society grows! . . . The history of the discovery of growth is a large part of the history of human culture. That individuals grow, that the child grows to be a man, the colt a horse, the scion a tree, is easily recognized, though with unassisted eye the processes of growth are not discovered. But that races grow—races of men, races of animals, races of plants, races or groups of worlds—is a very late discovery, and yet all of us do not grasp so great a thought. (3–4)

If the thought that races of men, animals, plants, or worlds "grow" was lost on most who early-on studied American Indian world versions, the thought that Native opinions were "childish" and "savage" was not. And so, the interactions between whites and Indians—where the principal white concern was finding a solution to the "Indian Problem" through warfare, removal, assimilation, and even the termination and nonrecognition of some tribes—served to attack, weaken, and ultimately erase much of the oral tradition that preserved the "childish opinions" of the American Indians.[5] As a result, the older sources we have—the ones closer to unadulterated Native thought—consist of ethnographers like the scornful Powell and apologists like the sympathetic Neihardt interpreting a rapidly vanishing Indian world

version, as well as assimilated Indians like Dakota Charles Eastman and
Shawnee Thomas Wildcat Alford, who adopted "the way of civilization."
In each case, whether because of disdain, admiration, or assimilation, the
reliability of older sources must be trusted with caution.

The state of more recent sources may be even more problematic, as
Vine Deloria (2004) argues. "When we speak of American Indian philosophy today," he observes, "we are probably talking about several generations
of Indian people who have *popular* notions of what Indian philosophy might
have been, . . .' " but only a scant knowledge of old beliefs and ceremonies (4;
emphasis added). And although I am not as skeptical about the knowledge
of our elders as Deloria, I take his point that because of "the rush toward
assimilation" over the past forty years, the elders—our traditional source
of Native culture and values—may recall the boarding school days of the
1920s, the Great Depression and the 1950s revival of ceremonies, but "would
know little else of importance." Moreover, as a result of the stereotypical
portrayal of American Indians in contemporary popular culture—movies,
Castanedian "teachings" and the like—"things 'Indian' have become more
fantasy than real" (4–5). If so, then more contemporary accounts of Native
culture, religion, and beliefs may be even more unreliable than the older
sources recorded and interpreted by non-Natives.

The first sobering challenge, then, is how to regard the accuracy of
both old and new sources when developing an American Indian world version. Deloria recommends an intensive study of each while recognizing their
respective shortcomings, knowing ultimately that the best we may expect is a
"projection"—what I call a *rational reconstruction*—of a Native world version:
"The task today is that of intensive research and study to enable people *to
project* what the various tribal peoples *probably* meant when they described
the world around them" (4; emphasis added). Such is one reason why this will
be only one possible interpretation of American Indian philosophy, for there
are many other "projections" that are possible. It is a rational reconstruction,
and so must be judged on whether or not it plausibly accounts for a variety of
data, including linguistic studies, old ethnographies, anthropological observations, archeological speculations, interpreted Indian narratives, as well as the
work of contemporary Native and non-Native scholars, themselves trying to
reconstruct an American Indian world version.[6]

The second challenge to my project is even more sobering and is, perhaps, insurmountable, because of a fundamental contemporary constructivist
tenet: The pure content of sense experiences alone underdetermines the
ontology of the world. Instead, sense experiences are identified, categorized,
and ordered—*worlds are constructed*—through the use of language and other
symbol systems. In other words, there are no facts without a conceptualizing
intellect using some system of description, exemplification, or expression.
This constructivist tenet is explored with some care in the next chapter,

but one of its consequences important to this volume is that speakers of radically different languages—using radically different systems of identification, categorization, and ordering—will conceive of the world in radically different ways. *Different words make different worlds*. So, any translation of an American Indian language into a Western language, no matter how carefully or neutrally crafted, will recast Native thought into the conceptual categories—hence, the ontology—of the Western language. Indeed, I argue later that much of our talk about "spirits" in the Native world version makes this very mistake, giving American Indian beliefs an unwarranted air of mysticism in Western popular culture—and in the academy—because of the supernatural connotations of the Western category *spirit*.

I resisted the constructivist tenet that different languages construct different worlds early in my philosophical career, but nothing made its plausibility more evident than my attempts to learn Shawnee, one of the many Algonquin languages.[7] After several years of reflection, I have come to believe that native Shawnee speakers specifically, and the old Indians in general, lived in a radically different world than ours—a substantial claim this work seeks to support. Two brief bits of evidence suffice for now.

Consider first that European languages regard gender important enough to mark grammatically. All have gendered pronouns and possessives, and many—French, Spanish, and German among them—have gendered nouns, although no one can say exactly why "mouse"—*la souris*—should be feminine, whereas "cat"—*le chat*—is masculine. What is important, however, is that these linguistic traditions use gender categories to organize experience, and in so doing recognize and reinforce gender difference as one of the most fundamental distinctions in the Western world version and the world it constructs. Many American Indian languages like Shawnee use a syntactic device to mark a different sort of category, namely, the *animate*, recognizing and reinforcing the fundamental distinction between animate and inanimate entities in their worlds. Shawnee does so with an ending morpheme "–a," as in the nouns, "kweewa" (woman), "hanikwa" (squirrel), "weepikwa" (spider), and "sacouka" (flint) (Wagar, pers. comm.; Ridout 2006). Shawnee also uses the formative suffix "–θa" when referring to *persons*—with the ending morpheme "–a"—as in "wiyeeθa" (someone), "skoteeθa" (fire person), "nepiiθa" (water person), and "weepikwaθa" (spider person) (Voegelin 1939: 335). Again, as in the case of gender in European languages, what is important here is that Shawnee uses the categories "animate" and "inanimate" to organize experience, and in this way reinforces the difference between animated beings and those not animated as one of the most fundamental distinctions in the Shawnee's constructed world.[8]

Second, notice that European languages have one first-person plural pronoun, for example, the "we" of English, the *nous* of French and the *wir* of German. However, Shawnee has two first-person plural pronouns, the exclusive "niilape" and the inclusive "kiilape." If I were to say to you "saawa-nwa niilape," then I would be saying "We [excluding you] are Shawnee." On the other hand, if I were to say "saawanwa kiilape," then I would be saying "We [including you] are Shawnee." Now this difference is clearly expressible in English—I just did so—but unlike the gender distinction in English, it is not a difference fundamental enough to mark grammatically. However, in the Shawnee world the composition of a group or community—and how one stands with respect to the group—is critically important enough to be recognized and reinforced by two first-person plural pronouns.

These two bits of evidence will be buttressed by others, suggesting that speakers of American Indian languages—languages that use systems of identification, categorization, and ordering far different from Western languages—conceive of the world in radically different ways. As a consequence, translations of Native narratives into their Western counterparts will recast the fundamental ontological categories of the Native world version into Western categories, and so misinterpret American Indian ontological beliefs. For example, someone unaware of either the Shawnee grammatical mark for the animate category or the subtleties of the Shawnee pantheon of "dei-ties" might translate "tepe'ki kisaθwa" as "moon," masking that the "night luminary" is an entity that gives light, and is not only *animate* as the ending morpheme "–a" indicates, but is a powerful *person*.[9] "[The Shawnee] have no definite idea of the formation, size or shape of the sun or moon, but suppose them to be a man & a woman of immense power & size." (Trowbridge, in Kinietz and Voegelin 1939: 37).

On the other hand, a translation of a Native expression into a West-ern one may impute properties absent in the American Indian worldview, as in the translation of "neir" (from some unspecified American Indian language) as "wind." In his own inimitable inimical fashion, Powell (1877) recognizes and poses this challenge as one among many obstacles in "fully present[ing] . . . the condition of savagery":

> The . . . difficulty lies in the attempt to put savage thoughts into civilized language. Our words are so full of meaning, carry with them so many great thoughts and collateral ideas. In English I say *wind*, and you think of atmosphere in revolution with the earth, heated at the tropics and cooled at the poles, and set into great currents that are diverted from their courses in pass-ing back and forth from tropical to polar regions; you think of ten thousand complicating conditions by which local currents are produced, and the word suggests all the lore of the Weather Bureau—that great triumph of American science. But when I say *neir* to a savage, and he thinks of a great monster, a breathing beast beyond the mountains of the west. (5)

Expressed without Powell's effusive pride in Western civilization and scholarly contempt for Native traditions, we may take the point to be that translating the Native "neir" as "wind" stands in danger of imputing all of the "great thoughts and collateral ideas"—all of the *ontological baggage*—of the English understanding of "wind" to the Native "neir."

The second sobering challenge to my project should now be obvious: Using *any* non-Native translation cannot do full justice to the underlying ontological, epistemological, and axiological beliefs and values of the original Native world version. What's worse, my account to come—crafted in a non-Native language—cannot escape this same inherent difficulty. Thus, we have a second reason why my interpretation is, at best, a rational reconstruction of American Indian philosophy—just one among many possible interpretations. Taken together with the first challenge of distinguishing between reliable and suspect sources, our reflections on the constructivist tenet that "different words make different worlds" mandate that we proceed with extreme caution and with modest expectations for success. You may want to put this book down and start another.

Four Common Themes: A First Look

Donald Fixico (2003), an American Indian history professor, anticipates two of our four common themes in American Indian philosophy, *relatedness* and *circularity* as world-ordering principles, when he observes that:

> "Indian Thinking" is "seeing" things from a perspective emphasizing that circles and cycles are central to the world and that all things are related within the universe. . . . "Seeing" is visualizing the connection between two or more entities or beings, and trying to understand the relationship between them. (1–2)

Reserving our discussion of *circularity* for Chapter 7, Chapter 4 shows that *relatedness as a world-ordering principle*—visualizing or constructing relationships or connections between entities—has important implications for our understanding of Native ontology, verification, and knowledge. Indeed, Deloria (1999) characterizes relatedness as "a practical methodological tool for investigating the natural world" (34).

Deloria illustrates the American Indian views that "all things are related," and how it is used as an investigatory tool, by appealing to one of Luther Standing Bear's (2006) boyhood recollections:

> I also remember a small fruit or berry which grew in sandy soil on low bushes. When ripe, they were black like cherries, so white

> people called them 'sand cherries.' Our name for them was *e-un-ye-ya-pi*. There is something peculiar about these cherries. When we gathered them, we always stood against the wind and never with the wind blowing from us across the plant. If we did, the fruit lost some of its flavor, but if gathered in the right way, they were sweeter than if gathered in the wrong way. This, I believe, is one of the many secrets which the Indian possesses, for I have never met a white person who knew this. (12)

Deloria interprets this bit of Native knowledge about the harvesting of sand cherries as "unquestionable" evidence of a particular human–plant relationship, in which humans benefit if respectfully approaching the plant. Moreover, these kinds of "secrets" can be discovered when one investigates the natural world assuming that such relationships exist—that "all things are related" (34–38). However, I suggest here that such relationships in the American Indian world version are constructed rather than discovered—that relatedness is one way that Natives order sense experiences.

A good friend, Walter S. Smith, suggested a little exercise to give a Western mind a place to begin when first introduced to an American Indian worldview; I have modified it a bit to reflect my own understanding, but the idea is essentially his and I thank him here. Having used it in numerous classroom and community forums over the years, it almost has never failed to produce the same, predictable results. A group is first given twenty seconds to make a list of as many kinds of animals as possible, and then twenty seconds to make a list of as many kinds of persons as possible. The brief period of time for each task is supposed to elicit a reflexive rather than a considered response on the assumption that unreflective responses best reflect deeply ingrained conceptual categories. A typical list of kinds of animals sounds like "dog, cat, bird, fish, mouse, lion, tiger, and bear (oh my!)" with an occasional "aardvark," "rhinoceros," "triceratops," or even "zebra muscle." There is no typical list of kinds of persons, for there are many ways participants can interpret the request; indeed, for this reason, lists of persons are always much shorter than lists of animals, because, unlike the request for different kinds of animals, each participant must first decide just what she or he is being asked to list. Lists of kinds of persons tend to fall into three categories: human characteristics, human nationalities, and human ethnicities. A typical example of a list of human characteristics is "man, woman, bald, thin, and happy"; a typical list of nationalities is "American, Canadian, Mexican, and Irish"; and a list of human ethnicities usually runs "Caucasian, African American, Asia American, and Native American."

The interesting thing to note—and the thing that makes this an illuminating exercise when first introduced to an American Indian worldview—is that the one animal notably absent from typical lists of animals is "human being." Moreover, typical lists of persons have never included any nonhuman being. But why should this be surprising? After all, it is a deeply ingrained Western religious view that human beings are different in kind from animals by virtue of ensoulment, and it is a deeply ingrained Western scientific view that human beings are different in kind from animals by virtue of their highly advanced evolution, so it is unsurprising to find these prejudices reflected in participants' lists of animals. And because every Western academic discipline, religious doctrine, and barroom discussion assumes that being human is a necessary condition for personhood—assumes it almost as naturally as breathing—it is a most unremarkable occurrence that a list of persons would include nothing but human characteristics, nationalities or ethnicities. Traditional Native list makers, however, would include "human being" on the list of animals without a second thought, and, remarkably, would include nonhuman beings on the list of persons. Indeed, it would not be at all surprising if the list of animals were a subset of the list of persons.[10]

Our little exercise illustrates something that cultural anthropologists and ethnographers have often observed, namely, that human beings and other animals are in some sense "equal" in the American Indian world version. According to J. W. Powell (1877):

> There is another very curious and interesting fact in Indian philosophy. They do not separate man from the beast by any broad line of demarkation [sic]. Mankind is supposed simply to be one of the many races of animals; in some respects superior, in many others inferior, to those races. So the Indian speaks of "our race" as of the same rank with the bear race, the wolf race or the rattlesnake race. (10)

However, I argue in Chapter 5 that Powell and others misinterpret this "very curious and interesting fact." Human beings are not lowered to the status of other animals as Powell implies; instead, animals and other sorts of nonhuman beings are raised to the ontological and moral status of *person*. This expansive conception of persons is the second common theme explored here.

The third recurring theme across American Indian world versions, the semantic potency of performance, is considered in Chapter 6. My understanding of this component of the Native worldview—that performing with a symbol is the principal vehicle of meaning in Native traditions—was framed by Sam Gill (1982, 1987), and I thank him here. Gill's crucial insight is that an understanding of Native religions depends on an appreciation of American Indian oral traditions in which songs, prayers, ceremonies, and other sorts of performances—and not the written word—are the primary and the potent bearers of semantic content. The point extends from a narrow consideration of religion to the entire Native worldview, for we have seen that there are no sharp distinctions between various domains of human activity in American Indian world versions.

Gill (1982) observes that "[w]e live in a world in which writing is taken for granted," and that the written word "is central to our forms of government and economy, our society and material culture (i.e., the things we have), and certainly to our pursuit of knowledge and the ways in which culture is transmitted from generation to generation" (41–42). Indeed, the written word is so ubiquitous in the Western world that it dissolves into the background, becoming just another virtually indistinguishable feature of the environment.

A 1959 episode of Rod Serling's *The Twilight Zone* entitled "Time Enough at Last" illustrates the centrality and power of written language as a cornerstone of Western culture. Bespectacled bank teller Henry Bemis is addicted to reading, and his addiction gets him into trouble at home and at work. While spending his lunchtime reading in the bank vault, a nuclear attack takes place, leaving Bemis the sole survivor. Making his way to the library, Bemis stacks books by month, planning his reading schedule for years to come—Shakespeare and Shaw, Shelley and Keats. Bemis has "time enough at last" to read—but then he shatters his coke-bottle eyeglasses . . . ("The Twilight Zone" 2009). Irony aside, the important point here is that the last man on earth has access to the whole of Western culture—its philosophy and history, literature and science, religion and values—because the written word is its principal vehicle of meaning. Although we speak metaphorically about "having a conversation with an author" when reading, Gill (1982) is correct in observing that, "Writing and reading are usually private acts, done by oneself in isolation from others" (45).

This is manifestly not the case in American Indian oral traditions in which speech acts and other performances—either symbolic acts or actions with symbols—are the primary bearers of semantic content. As well, unlike communication in Western culture, oral traditions require some members of the community—the elders—to be repositories of knowledge and values, to preserve and transmit them across generations. Consider Black Elk (2000), for example, who was anguished at age seventeen because he still did not understand the great vision given to him eight years earlier, so his parents asked an elder for help:

> [M]y father and mother asked an old medicine man by the name
> of Black Road to come over and see what he could do for me.
> Black Road was in a tepee all alone with me, and he asked me
> to tell him if I had seen something that troubled me. By now

I was so afraid of everything that I told him about my vision, and when I was through he looked long at me and said: "Ah-h-h-h!," meaning that he was much surprised. Then he said to me: "Nephew, I know now what the trouble is! You must do what the bay horse in your vision wanted you to do. You must do your duty and perform this vision for your people upon earth. You must have the horse dance first for the people to see. Then the fear will leave you." (122–23)

Along with another old and wise elder, Bear Sings, Black Road helped Black Elk perform the horse dance from his vision for the people, and with its performance—ceremonial actions with symbols—the vision came to have meaning and power. But Black Elk could not have performed the vision in isolation; unlike Bemis—who needs no one to help him understand a book—Black Elk's understanding comes only with the help and wisdom of the elders. No wonder the forced removal of American Indians from their tribal lands was such a tragedy, for the harshest rigors of removal fell on the elders—the repositories of tribal knowledge and culture—many of whom did not survive. It would be as if we all forgot how to read and write, or, like Bemis, shattered our eyeglasses.

It is a commonplace that American Indians regard some places as sacred, for example, the Black Hills for the Lakota, the Petroglyph National Monument in New Mexico for Puebloan people, and the Hopewellian ceremonial complexes in Ohio like the Newark and Fort Ancient earthworks. And it is equally common to find both Native and non-Native authors alike proposing that the fundamental difference between Western and Indian religious traditions is that the former is framed by time, sacred events, and history while the latter focuses on space, sacred places, and nature. Deloria (1994) makes the point this way:

When the domestic ideology is divided according to the American Indian and Western European immigrant . . . the fundamental difference is one of great philosophical importance. American Indians hold their lands—places—as having the highest possible meaning, and all of their statements are made with this reference point in mind. Immigrants review the movement of their ancestors across the continent as a steady progression of basically good events and experiences, thereby placing history—time—in the best possible light. (62)

However, in Chapter 7 I argue that there is a more fundamental distinction to be drawn, one that supports the difference between Western time and

Native place. Fixico again anticipates the difference between the American Indian way of "seeing and thinking" and its Western counterpart by explaining that Natives "see" things from a perspective emphasizing *circularity*, while the Western mind is *linear*. Hence, the last common theme in American Indian world versions we consider is *circularity as a world-ordering principle*.

By the way, if circles and cycles—and not lines and linear progressions—are central to a way of constructing the American Indian world, then the iron-fisted one-dimensional temporal progression that rules over the Western mind and world will not hold sway over Native peoples; they are neither obsessed with nor driven by linear time as are their Western counterparts.[11]

This is not to deny, of course, that "Indians hold their lands—places—as having the highest possible meaning," that is, *sacredness*. Indeed, in the sanctity of particular places we find yet another reason why the forced removal of American Indians from their tribal lands was so devastating. Without doubt, there are sacred sites in Western religions, for example, the purported site of the birth of Jesus, where now stands the Church of the Nativity. However, Christianity could get along quite well without knowing about these places, for events are more important than places in the Christian tradition. But without the event of the Resurrection, there simply would be no Christianity. In Native religious traditions, place is more sacred than an event, although a place can be sanctified by an event that occurred at that site (Deloria 1994: 267–82). So, removal for American Indians was not a mere trade of occupied tribal lands for other land elsewhere. Removal separated Native people from their sacred places, the consequence of which would be as devastating as separating a Christian from the event of the Resurrection, if such a thing were possible.

Constructing an Actual American Indian World

Here we have, then, a first look at the four common themes we consider in this interpretation of American Indian philosophy as the dance of person and place: relatedness and circularity as world-ordering principles, the expansive conception of persons, and the semantic potency of performance. But presenting such an interpretation of a Native philosophical worldview is just a part of my current project. I argue as well that from a culturally sophisticated constructivist perspective grounded in the philosophy of Nelson Goodman, an American Indian world version constructs an actual, well-made world.

Since first contact with the indigenous peoples of the Americas, the Western intellectual tradition has sometimes regarded Native worldviews as interesting and rich subjects of anthropological study, but almost always as

primitive and uncivilized, false and empty, and very often as moral abomina-
tions to be extinguished. Lewis Hanke's (1959) analysis of the great debate
in Valladolid in 1550 between Juan Ginés de Sepúlveda and Bartolomé
de las Casas shows that there was never doubt about the moral inferiority
of the Native worldview, but only about whether or not Indians have an
Aristotelian "slave nature." If so, as Sepúlveda argued, then it is right to
Christianize them through warfare; if not, as las Casas argued, they could be
converted without warfare. The obvious goal in either case was to compel
Native people to abandon their false and morally corrupt beliefs.

About three hundred years later, ethnographer Powell (1877) offered
a scholarly assessment of the ethical value of "Indian theology":

> The literature of North American ethnography is vast, and scat-
> tered through it is a great mass of facts pertaining to Indian theol-
> ogy—a mass of nonsense, a mass of incoherent folly . . . ethically
> a hideous monster of lies, but ethnographically a system of great
> interest—a system which beautifully reveals the mental condi-
> tion of savagery. (13)

In 1907 ethnographer L. T. Hobhouse offered a similar opinion about
the lack of Western metaphysical distinctions in Native worldviews:

> primitive thought has not yet evolved those distinctions of
> substance and attribute, quality and relation, cause and effect,
> identity and difference, which are the common property of
> civilized thought. These categories which among us every child
> soon comes to distinguish in practice are for primitive thought
> interwoven in wild confusion.(Gilmore 1919: 20-21)

Unsurprisingly, these kinds of "scholarly" views about Native worldviews provided one rationale among many for the U.S. government's policy of
forced assimilation between the late 1880s and mid-1930s, designed to "civi-
lize" American Indians—to "kill the Indian and save the man," as Richard
Henry Pratt famously put it. "Civilizing" American Indians—ridding Native
peoples of their primitive thought and savage ways—required the destruction
of Indian cultures and art, the banning of Native religious ceremonies, the
allotment of tribal lands, and the placement of children in boarding schools
where they were unable to speak their native tongue (Beck, 2001).

Our respected philosophical contemporaries are no less dismissive
of the Native worldview. W. V. O. Quine (1960) speculated that among
the "disreputable origins" of dubious discourse about abstract objects are
"confusions over mass terms, confusions of sign and object, perhaps even *a*

savage theology"—a witticism, perhaps, from an engaging writer; but I believe we know Quine's answer were he asked whether or not a Native version of the world is false or empty (123, emphasis added). Goodman (1984), himself, uses a Native commonplace to illustrate the view that not all world versions are true: "[A]fter all," he writes, "some versions say the earth . . . *rests on the back of a tortoise*" (30, emphasis added).

Now, a fundamental Goodmanian constructivist tenet is that a world is "well made" and actual only if it is constructed by a true version, so if a world version is false or empty, then there will be no well-made, actual world created by it. And, assuming that ill-made or unmade worlds are of little philosophical interest, scant philosophical value will be found in a Native worldview if it turns out to be false or empty—as the prevailing Western attitude has it. Anthropological voyeurism aside, what of philosophical importance will there be to discover in the American Indian world version? Clearly, one of my present purposes must be to show that the prevailing western attitude is incorrect, and that an American Indian world version is neither false nor empty, and so constructs an actual, well-made world. This task is begun in Chapter 2 with the introduction of important tenets of Goodman's constructivist view, including (1) the view that facts are fabricated by world versions, (2) the doctrine of ontological pluralism, that there are many internally consistent, equally privileged, well-made *actual* worlds, (3) the criteria for an ultimately acceptable world version, and (4) the view that ultimately acceptability is sufficient for truth, and true versions construct well-made actual worlds.

Chapter 3 begins the argument for the legitimacy of an American Indian world version from a constructivist perspective, beginning with an argument in favor of a constructive *realism* rather than Goodman's constructive *nominalism*. I then argue that Goodman's criteria for the ultimate acceptability of a world version are culturally biased, so they beg the question against any non-Western world version, especially an American Indian world version. However, a culturally sophisticated reinterpretation of Goodman's criteria should find an American Indian world numbered among the internally consistent, equally privileged, well-made actual worlds.

Chapter 4 concludes the argument for the legitimacy of an American Indian world version from a culturally sophisticated constructivist perspective through an examination of a Native conception of knowledge, for truth and verification within an American Indian world version are important to understanding the culturally informed criteria for an ultimately acceptable version. And, given that ultimate acceptability is sufficient for truth, and that true versions construct well-made actual worlds, I conclude that an American Indian world is, indeed, numbered among the internally consistent, equally privileged, well-made actual worlds and so it is worthy of philosophical treatment—and respect—from the Western perspective.

2

Nelson Goodman's Constructivism

This chapter rehearses important tenets of Nelson Goodman's constructivist view that there is a plurality of internally consistent, equally privileged, well-made *actual* worlds constructed through the use of very special symbol systems—true or right-world versions. It pays special attention to world-constructing processes and to Goodman's criteria for an ultimately acceptable world version.

Setting the Stage

On a fine spring morning in May I looked out the kitchen window and saw some critters around the backyard bird feeder. I drew a picture of them (Figure 2.1). Now, I'm no ornithologist, but I am a fairly competent at

Figure 2.1. My backyard bird feeder

identifying backyard flora and fauna. The morning light was bright, my eyesight was not impaired, and the distinctive red color, black eye-patch and topnotch were together a dead giveaway. The *fact* is that there were three cardinals around the feeder. That fact makes *true* the statement that there were three cardinals around the feeder; and, given that my true belief is justified, I *know* that there were three cardinals around the feeder. (And yes, that *is* an eastern gray squirrel on the woodpile in the distance, so you know what happened in the next little bit; but let's ignore her for now.)

This would be a very short chapter, were this—the naïve realist view— the whole story. By the way, calling "naïve" the view that there is a mind-independent world of *facts* to which our true statements correspond is not to imply that it's foolish. Indeed, except at our most reflective moments, it is our everyday way of thinking about and being in the world.

Here are some more *facts* with their corresponding *truths*: The cardinal on the feeder was red; there were two cardinals on the ground; there was one natural kind—the cardinal—exemplified by the birds around the feeder; there were three pairs of cardinal legs, eyes, and wings; there were no persons around the feeder; the feeder contained more sunflower seeds than the number of birds atop it; the feeder was not moving; it is the same feeder I installed fifteen years ago; twenty seconds later there was one eastern gray—and no cardinals—at the feeder.

Remarkably, my stationary bird feeder with its avian guests was also moving at a blazing 67,000 miles per hour, the speed at which the Earth races around the sun (NASA 2005). Trusting the veracity of NASA astrophysicists—especially about the motion of the Earth—we have to explain how two contradictory statements, "The bird feeder did not move" and "The bird feeder moved," are true in virtue of two competing facts. I reject out of hand, by the way, that the *real* fact of the matter is that the Earth is racing at a reckless speed, so that my belief that the feeder did not move is really *false*. For I have as much evidence for a stationary Earth as did Aristotle: Neither I nor my feeder is moving. I am not advocating a return to a pre-Copernican view of planetary motion; nor am I interested in embracing the multimillennial distinction between appearance and reality—that is, it *appears* to be stationary, but it's *really* moving. "Knock, knock, Neo" (Wachowski Brothers 1999). Instead, I side with the view called constructivism, which maintains that the notion of a mind-independent world of facts is mistaken, because a fact is "fabricated," as Nelson Goodman (1978) famously put it. Truth, understood as a correspondence relation between statements and mind-independent facts, fairs little better.

Constructivism is not new, and its many adherents have understood the constructivist claim in a variety of ways, moving away from the Kantian view that sense experiences are ordered by innate and universal mental processes to an understanding that sense experiences are categorized and ordered by language and other symbol systems. Notable contemporary philosophers sounding a constructivist theme include Thomas Kuhn, W. V. O. Quine, Philip Kitcher, and Hilary Putnam. However, I am especially fond of Goodman's constructivist account. Indeed, with a few realist modifications some will find heretical—but we're all friends here—I believe that the resulting view I call *constructive realism* is even more plausible. Moreover, I argue that a culturally sophisticated reinterpretation of Goodman's view will find an American Indian world numbered among the internally consistent, equally privileged, well-made actual worlds.

Fact, Fiction, and Feeders

My consideration of Goodman's views focuses on four major interconnected themes developed over the course of his philosophical career:

(i)   the speciousness of the *bare fact*—the *pure given*—as an epistemological foundation, and the construction of worlds through the use of symbol systems called *world versions*;

(ii) an ontological pluralism, that is, the existence of many ontologically diverse, yet equally privileged constructed actual worlds;

(iii) the use of pragmatic criteria in judging truth and the construction of well-made worlds by true versions; and

(iv) nonliteral versions and the advancement of understanding.

Goodman (1978) begins his account in *Ways of Worldmaking* at a place very much similar to our own, wondering how the apparently contradictory statements, "The sun always moves" and "The sun never moves" can both be true without logically implying the truth of every other statement. His answer is that each of the statements is true relative to a different frame of reference—a version or description of the world. That is, under a geocentric frame of reference (the frame evidenced by our everyday way of experiencing the world) the sun always moves, and under a heliocentric frame of reference (the frame employed by NASA) the sun never moves. The first of Goodman's (1978) crucial insights is that these "[f]rames of reference . . . seem to belong less to what is described than to systems of descriptions" (2). A "system of description"—*a world version*—is grounded in the categorization and ordering of sense experiences employing linguistic symbols; that is, a version of the world is grounded in the fabrication of facts through the devices of a language.

The speciousness of the *bare fact* as an epistemological foundation—compellingly argued by Berkeley and especially by Kant—is a common theme in contemporary constructivist thought, for the pure content of sense experiences alone underdetermines how the world *really* is. Indeed, as Goodman argues (using a decidedly Berkeleyan argument), one cannot even describe what the *pure given* might be apart from the order or structure imposed by a description, for, of course, one must employ a description in the account.[1] "Talk of unstructured content or an unconceptualized given or a substratum without properties is self-defeating; for the talk imposes structure, conceptualizes, ascribes properties" (6). Thus, the question of whether my feeder is *really* moving or not is empty, for without a conceptualizing intellect using a system of description, there is no fact.

One of my favorite ways to illustrate the fabrication of facts rehearses René Descartes' (1993) classic argument about a piece of wax in *Meditations on First Philosophy*. Recall that Descartes begins with a piece of beeswax with its usual honeycomb appearance, and upon heating, changes its appearance in every respect. And yet, the Cartesian rationalist can know the mind-independent bare facts that, although the wax has changed in appearance in every respect, it is the *same* wax after heating as before, and that, as an extended material body, the wax is "capable of innumerable changes" in shape and volume—and these facts are supposedly known *a priori* by virtue of an innate idea about the nature of material substance (21–24). But without the aid of mysterious Cartesian innate ideas or their contemporary counterparts, one wonders how knowledge about such bare facts as the duration of material objects over time—even when their appearances change in every respect—is possible. After all, why shouldn't *a different appearance evidence a different thing?* Indeed, in the vast majority of cases, a different appearance *does* evidence a different thing—and sometimes even when the two things occupy the same spatial location in temporal sequence.[2]

However, it would be entirely consistent with the content of Descartes' sense experiences if, upon changing the appearance of the wax in every respect, he judged that the wax did *not* remain the same material substance throughout the experiment at all, but in "fact" was replaced by *different* stuff. Indeed, we might imagine this being the judgment made by Descartes' fictional twin sister, Renee, who was spirited away at birth and raised in an ontological tradition wherein a different appearance *always* evidences a different thing and there are some shapes material substance cannot assume. But, if sense experiences cannot alone settle these ontological issues—whether or not a material object endures through various changes in appearance and can assume innumerable shapes—what could?

We've already hinted at the answer. There is no *bare fact* of the matter to be grasped by some mysterious epistemic process. What Descartes believed to be *a priori* knowledge about material substance actually had a linguistic component—his conception of material substance mirrored his linguistic community's as contained in and conveyed by its talk about physical objects. Beginning with the content of similar sense experiences but inheriting radically different talk about physical objects—a radically different version of the world—fictional Renee believed that an object is destroyed when its appearance changes in every respect and that material substance is incapable of changing into some shapes. Perhaps these culturally instilled beliefs about physical objects were such a habit of mind that Renee believed them to be known *a priori*. However, the content of our twins' similar sense experiences alone cannot establish how the world of material substance *really* is—or even, *as Berkeley doubted, whether the world is composed of material substance!*

Now, if the content of our sense experiences underdetermines reality, then there are many possible versions of my backyard world that are consistent with my experiences—but which sound very odd—for English speakers bring a particular linguistically informed ontological interpretation to the scene. Observe that in this simple case we use expressions like "a cardinal," "my feeder," and "the squirrel in the distance" to denote enduring individual material entities; we use predicates like "red," "two," "same," and "person," and prepositions like "atop" to denote properties of and relations between such entities; finally, we treat "moves" as an intransitive verb. However, in a frame of reference wherein "red" is regarded as an intransitive verb like "moves," the statement "The cardinal atop the feeder redded" is true. In another frame employing the predicate "grue" (where a thing is grue if it is either green or blue) it is true that "The cardinal atop the feeder was not grue."[3] It is true in a nominalist frame that "There were three individual cardinals at the feeder, but no abstract natural kind—the cardinal—they exemplified." If we suppose a frame of reference wherein "cardinal" is a mass term like "water" or "gold," then it is true that "There was cardinal at the feeder." We've already seen that "The feeder moved" is a fact according to NASA's heliocentric frame of reference. René might say "It is the same feeder installed 15 years ago," while Renee might swear that it's different. Finally, in a Quine-inspired (1960) frame of reference wherein material objects come in short temporal slices, it is true that "later there were no cardinals, but many eastern grays at the feeder" (26–79). These are some odd facts indeed, for most contradict our habit of thinking and talking about the world, our preferred linguistically categorized and ordered frame of reference—*but not one of them is inconsistent with the content of our sense experiences.*

Although curious to a Western ontological conception of the world, some of these *facts* and their corresponding *truths* are very much at home in Native versions. Algonquin languages like Shawnee, lacking the verb "to be," treat English adjectives like "red" as intransitive verbs (Wagar, pers. comm.). So, a Shawnee speaker commenting on my backyard scene might say *meci skwaawa*, expressing about the cardinals the fact that "They redded." As well, the Shawnee stem "skipaky-" applies to a thing if it is either blue or green—or better said, if the thing either blues or greens.[4] Observe that Voegelin (1939) translates "ni*skipaki*to" as "I made it blue" and "*skipaki*seeya" "green cloth" (314). Perhaps most remarkable difference between Western and Native frames is this: Although "There were no persons around the feeder" is true in the Western version, in the Native frame of reference the fact is that there were three persons around the feeder—until the eastern gray arrived, of course, and then there was only a single person dining.

Granting the speciousness of the *pure given*, more must be said about how Goodman (1978) believes worlds are constructed through the use of symbol systems. Especially noteworthy is his careful analysis of the construction of versions through both linguistic and nonlinguistic systems. Important at the outset is the observation that worlds, and the objects and kinds that comprise those worlds, are not created from scratch, but are recreations from other worlds. "The many stuffs—matter, energy, waves, phenomena—that worlds are made of are made along with the worlds. But made from what? Not from nothing, but from other worlds . . . the making is a remaking" (6).

Denotation, the relation between a symbol and what the symbol stands for or refers to, is the fundamental relation in world making, for the application of labels—names, predicates, gestures, pictures, and so on—identifies the objects and kinds that comprise a world by ordering and categorizing the content of sense experiences. The name "Abby Wallace" is a label denoting my pet squirrel, serving to consolidate temporally disparate yet similar experiences into an enduring entity; she is the *same* squirrel this morning as the starving dray who crawled onto my shoe five years ago. "Eastern gray" is a predicate label with multiple denotation, standing for all of the individual squirrels in its extension, and organizing the world into a relevant class of things—a *natural* kind (Goodman 1984: 36). The predicate "green" likewise organizes the world into a color kind in a way different from the Shawnee stem "skipaky-." And to one who is color deficient, there are far more objects in the extension of the predicate "green" than to one with usual color vision; "green" for the former would be something like the union of the extensions of the predicates "green," "orange," "tan," and "beige" for the latter. But such labeling takes place neither piecemeal nor in isolation; denotation always occurs against the backdrop of an established ontology sustained by past linguistic practice. As we've seen, English speakers use "a squirrel" to stand for an enduring individual material entity, not temporal stages of squirrels, undetached squirrel parts, an amount of squirrel mass, or even squirrelhood.

When speaking about the world of backyard flora and fauna, our frame of reference assumes the object ontology of naïve realism.

Goodman (1978) considers several world-constructing processes, but he cautions that his list is neither comprehensive nor exhaustive. Indeed, his modest goal is to "suggest something of the variety of processes in constant use" (17). Importantly, although Goodman asserts that a "tighter system-atization" of processes for constructing new worlds from old is possible, he denies that any such systematization will be "ultimate," "for there is no more a unique world of worlds than there is a unique world" (17). However, I argue here that a multiplicity of equally privileged constructed worlds does not imply a multiplicity of equally privileged world-constructing processes; a relativity of worlds does not imply a relativity of *ways* of constructing them. (A vast number of different wooden structures can be built with a single set of tools: saws, hammers, squares, levels, etc.) In fact, I maintain that there are *kinds* of world-constructing activities—with *kinds* understood not as Goodman's relevant classes but as a realist does. But there is much more to do before that case can be made.

Four of the most common world-making processes Goodman discuss-es are composition, decomposition, weighting, and ordering, all of which depend on—and help to determine—how the world is organized into objects and kinds. Composition is a process of uniting in a new version of the world what were before apparently distinct objects or kinds, such as the uniting of the morning star and the evening star under the label "Venus," with the resulting identification of the two objects and the fabrication of the new fact: The morning star is the *same* thing as the evening star. "Effects of global warming" labels a collection of diverse climatic phenomena, including glacial melting, changing precipitation patterns, intensified storms, and the northern march of flora and fauna. Decomposition is an opposite process, the dissolution of objects into distinct parts or the partitioning of kinds into subspecies (Goodman 1978: 7), as exemplified by Voegelin's (1939) transla-tion of the Shawnee stem "nooc'-" as "teasing, flirting or fighting" (377), or the subcategorization of the everyday kind "squirrel" into the biological family sciuridae—and into its five subfamilies, eighty-one genera, and hun-dreds of species (Myers et al. 2008).

The explanation of weighting, a third prominent process of world construction, is grounded in the observation that any two things have some property or feature in common, and so are members of a kind determined by that common feature in some world version or other. Consider two entities that are seemingly different in every respect, say, a performance of Beethoven's Opus 80 "Choral Fantasy" and the "answer to the Ultimate Question of Life, the Universe and Everything"—the number 42 (Adams 1987: 465). And yet, they both have at least one thing in common, namely,

I have chosen them to be considered, so they are members of the kind "things chosen to illustrate that any two things have something in common." I anticipate the likely objection that kinds are determined by some essential feature exemplified by its members, but being presently chosen as an illustration is merely accidental. But why believe that? For present purposes and in this context there is nothing at all accidental about being chosen; indeed, it is the *only* feature that matters. In short, what counts as an essential feature—and so, in turn, a kind of thing—is a function of our organization and categorization of objects and kinds in a particular world version.

Depending on the predicate we specify, consider the various constructed kinds to which the elements in the grid of numerals (Figure 2.2) belong. Here is a mere handful: {x / x is an even number} = {2, 4, 6}; {x / x is a prime number} = {2, 3, 5}; {x / x is the additive inverse of −7} = { };{x / x is a red numeral} = {'1', '3'}; {x / x is a numeral in italics} = {'2', '3', '5'}; {x / x is a numeral in the right hand column of the grid} = {'1', '5'}; {x / "green" applies to x} = {'4', '5'}; {x / "skipakyi" applies to x} = {'2', '4', '5', '6'}; and {x / x is the number of numerals in the grid} = {6}. Each kind of thing depends on how the complex is regarded; each kind is constructed given the specified predicate. These kinds have no more an existence independent of an organizing and categorizing system than the objects comprising them.

But, of course, not all of the objects or kinds that can be constructed have a useful or familiar place in a particular world version; indeed, some kinds will be downright unwelcome, as is the case with the one determined by Goodman's (1983) predicate "grue." "Grue" applies to all things examined before time *t* just in case they are green but to other things just in case they are blue. Briefly, the well-known problem is that every observation of an emerald before time *t* confirms the general hypothesis that all emeralds

Red	Blue	Red
3	6	1
Blue	Green	Green
2	4	*5*

Figure 2.2. A grid of numerals

are green. But why doesn't each and every one of those observations likewise confirm the general hypothesis that all emeralds are grue? We clearly do not want to make predictions about grue things, as we do about things that are green; we do not believe that "grue" is projectible. The challenge, then, is to distinguish between hypotheses that are projectible (i.e., confirmed by evidence) and those that are not. Notice, importantly, that the problem is *not* that there is something particularly odious about the predicate "grue," for its relative "blite" is perfectly projectible. The predicate "blite" applies to all things in Europe examined before time t just in case they are white and to other things if they are observed to be either black or white. In this case, t just happens to be the exact moment on or about January 10, 1697, when Willem de Vlamingh discovered a black swan on the Swan River in western Australia ("Willem de Vlamingh" 2003). Before time t, every observation of a white swan confirmed that all swans are blite—*but not, remarkably, that all swans are white!*

Weighting as a world-constructing process is Goodman's solution to the problem of distinguishing projectible from nonprojectible predicates. Not all kinds are relevant in a particular world; green and white are relevant in our everyday world version, but grue and blite are not. That is, the kinds green and white are weighted more heavily than grue and blite, and they are so because they have become better *entrenched*. Predicates and the kinds they determine become entrenched principally as a result of actual past projections. "Plainly 'green,' as a veteran of earlier and many more projections than 'grue,' has the more impressive biography. The predicate 'green,' we may say, is much better *entrenched* than the predicate 'grue' " (Goodman 1983: 94). Entrenchment also serves to minimize the relevance of some predicates and their corresponding kinds. "Green" is better entrenched than "grue," and the projections "all emeralds are green" and "all emeralds are grue" conflict in their predictions about unobserved emeralds after time t (96). In cases of such conflict, the entrenched predicate carries the day and is deemed more relevant. So, while true that "all swans are blite," but false that "all swans are white," the projections conflict to the detriment of the unentrenched "blite."

Constructing a world using the process of weighting, of sorting relevant and irrelevant kinds, *creates regularities*—perhaps one of the most startling constructivist insights. Indeed, regularities are where you find them. All emeralds are green, but not all are grue; not all swans are white, but all are blite; all emeralds and cardinals are gred; "skipakyi"—"It blues or greens"—is true of the sky and grass. "The uniformity of nature we marvel at or the unreliability we protest belongs to a world of our own making" (Goodman 1978: 10).

Let us return to the grid (Figure 2.2) to discuss *ordering*, the final world-constructing process we consider. Ordering creates patterns, as the following few ways to order the six elements illustrate. Ordering by increasing and decreasing magnitudes, the patterns are "1, 2, 3, 4, 5, 6" and "6, 5, 4, 3, 2, 1," respectively. If we order the elements by increasing size of the numerals, we have "4, 6, 1, 3, 5, 2." If the grid is read left to right as English, then the pattern is "3, 6, 1, 2, 4, 5"; if read as Hebrew, "1, 6, 3, 5, 4, 2." The pattern is "3, 1, 4, 5, 2, 6," if we order the grid elements according to the first occurrence of the numerals in the decimal expansion of pi. And we can order by craps come out roll winning pairs: "1–6, 2–5, 3–4." We create patterns as we create regularities; patterns—like regularities—are where you find them.

Importantly, Goodman (1978) reminds us that an ordering is necessary for all measurement—a common way of manufacturing facts. Whether measuring distances in miles or kilometers, area in acres or hectares, volume in gallons or liters, or even temperature in Fahrenheit or Celsius, it is first necessary to construct the applicable metric, which requires specifying an ordering. In fact, measurement involves several world-making processes, as the measurement of temperature illustrates—or better said, how our *construction of facts about temperature* illustrates. We must first specify the denotation of "one degree"—the unit of measurement—after which an ordered metric is established. Note, importantly, that in the fabrication of facts through the process of measurement both the scale and the measuring device contribute. In measuring temperature, the choice of the Fahrenheit scale over the Celsius scale enables more distinctions in temperature to be created, for the former has 180 degree increments between freezing and boiling, whereas the latter has a mere 100 degree increments. Moreover, measuring temperature using an analogue rather than a digital device allows for even finer discrimination; although I might be able to judge the temperature to be between 42° and 43° using an analogue thermometer, there is no increment between 42° and 43° on its digital counterpart.

Again, this brief consideration of four world-constructing processes—composition, decomposition, weighting, and ordering—is incomplete; indeed, there are more ways of remaking new worlds from old Goodman (1978) discusses, viz., deletion, supplementation, and deformation. But we need not tarry, for we have sufficiently illustrated his views about the speciousness of the *bare fact* as an epistemological foundation and the construction of worlds through the use of symbol systems.

Ontological Pluralism

We have already seen that the content of our sense experiences underdetermines the way the world really is, so there are many possible interpretations—world versions—of the events taking place in my backyard—if, of course, events are a part of your linguistically informed ontology. Were "red" regarded as an intransitive verb, then the cardinals redded; in another world version, the cardinals are not grue; and there was cardinal at the feeder—but waters in various receptacles about the yard—were "cardinal" a mass term, but "water" not; and in the heliocentric frame the feeder moved, but in the geocentric it did not. But to say that there are many possible interpretations does not well express Goodman's (1983) view, for he famously argues that statements about the possible may be analyzed as statements about the actual, and that our conception of a *possible world* should be adjusted:

> What we often mistake for the actual world is one particular description of it. And what we mistake for possible worlds are just equally true descriptions in other terms. We have come to think of the actual as one among many possible worlds. We need to repaint that picture. All possible worlds lie within the actual one. (57)

Goodman's view that there are many *actual* ontologically diverse, yet equally privileged constructed worlds is called *ontological pluralism*. Ontological pluralism rests on the premise that there is no world independent of any particular representation, model, theory, or version we have of it. Instead, all of the characteristics of the world—the things we understand to be objects and kinds—are relative to a particular theory. Hilary Putnam is another champion of this view called *ontological relativity*, and he gives two arguments in its favor.[5] The first, which we here rehearse, observes that there are a number of ways of modeling a state of affairs depending on the features one considers to be important or extraneous. For example, if we focus on certain features of electromagnetic radiation, we construct the theory of light as a wave, which explains refraction and diffusion. Focusing on other features yields the theory of light as a particle, which explains the photoelectric effect. But as we saw earlier with my moving yet stationary feeder, the statement "Electro-magnetic radiation travels as photons" is true in the latter, but false in the former. Thus, Putnam concludes, being a photon is theory-relative (Norton-Smith 1985: 493–94). We may make the same point by considering the multiple isomorphic set-theoretic reductions of the natural numbers. Whereas the statement "The number 2 is $\{\{\phi\}\}$" is true in Zermelo's model, it is false in von Neumann's, in which it is true that "The number 2 is $\{\phi, \{\phi\}\}$." So, being the number 2 is relative to a particular model of the natural numbers. Indeed, even I proposed my preferred interpretation, arguing that the number 2 is a *collective kind* demarcated by an analogue of the standard criterion for the numerical equivalence of sets (Norton-Smith 1991).

Again, Goodman holds that there are many *actual* ontologically diverse, yet equally privileged constructed world versions. In the case of the multiple interpretations of first-order number theory, it is unimportant that these various ontologically diverse interpretations posit as primitives different sorts of objects or even that the models are mathematically isomorphic (i.e., there are bijective mappings from each to the others). Instead, the privilege comes from preserving a global isomorphism of structure between right versions—an extensional isomorphism—which the following seeks to illustrate.[6]

Consider the Venn diagram from your first formal logic class, used there to test the validity of categorical syllogisms. Remember, the idea is that there are three intersecting circles in a universe of discourse (Figure 2.3). This system we'll call the "SMP system," takes as undefined primitives the circular regions S, M, and P, the rectangular region U, and "contains" as the primitive relation. For any regions x and y, x is a subregion of y, written "x $\subset$ y," if and only if region y contains all of region x. So, for example, S $\subset$ U. Write "x $\in$ y" if and only if region y does not contain all of region x, so, for example, U $\in$ S. For any regions x and y, define the intersection of x and y, written "x $\cap$ y" as the subregion contained by both x and y. For any regions x and y, define the union of x and y, written "x $\cup$ y," as region formed by combining the regions x and y. Finally, define the complement of a region x, written "$\neg$x" as the subregion of U that does not contain any of x.

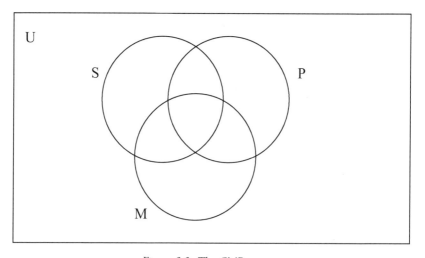

Figure 2.3. The SMP-system

Now, given this description of the SMP system we can express some facts about how the regions and subregions are related to each other. Here are a few:

(i) $(S \cap (M \cap P)) \subset S$, that is, region S contains the intersection of regions S, M, and P;

(ii) $(\neg S \cap (M \cap P)) \subset M$, that is, region M contains the intersection of regions $\neg S$, M, and P;

(iii) $(S \cap (\neg M \cap \neg P)) \subset \neg P$, that is, region $\neg P$ contains the intersection of regions S, $\neg M$, and $\neg P$;

(iv) $(S \cap (\neg M \cap P)) \in M$, that is, region M does not contain $S \cap (\neg M \cap P)$;

(v) $[(\neg S \cap (\neg M \cap P)) \cup (M \cap (\neg S \cap \neg P))] \in S$, that is, region S does not contain the union of regions $\neg S \cap (\neg M \cap P)$ and $M \cap (\neg S \cap \neg P)$.

In the second system (Figure 2.4), called the "8 system," the primitives are the eight regions designated by the numerals "1" through "8," and "contains" is the primitive relation; the focus here is on the eight disjoint regions that are created by the three intersecting circles. The following definitions mirror those for our SMP system: for any regions x and y, x is a subregion of y, written "$x \subset y$," if and only if region y contains all

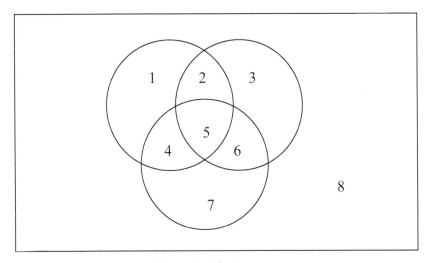

Figure 2.4. The 8-system

of region x. Write "x ∈ y" if and only if region y does not contain all of region x. For any regions x and y, define the intersection of x and y, written "x ∩ y" as the subregion contained by both x and y. For any regions x and y, define the union of x and y, written "x ∪ y" as region formed by combining the regions x and y. Although these are binary relationships, we'll relax the convention regarding parentheses in order to keep their proliferation under control. (This means we will write "Region (1 ∪ 2 ∪ 3 ∪ 4 ∪ 5 ∪ 6 ∪ 7 ∪ 8) comprises the entire rectangular region.") Finally, define the complement of a region x, written "¬x" as the subregion of (1 ∪ 2 ∪ 3 ∪ 4 ∪ 5 ∪ 6 ∪ 7 ∪ 8) that does not contain any of x.

Now, given this description of the 8 system we can express facts about how the regions and subregions are related to each other. Here are a few:

(i)   5 ⊂ (1 ∪ 2 ∪ 4 ∪ 5), that is, the union of the regions 1, 2, 4, and 5 contains region 5;

(ii) 6 ⊂ (4 ∪ 5 ∪ 6 ∪ 7), that is, the union of regions 4, 5, 6, and 7 contains region 6;

(iii) 1 ⊂ (1 ∪ 4 ∪ 7 ∪ 8), that is, the union of regions 1, 4, 7, and 8 contains region 1;

(iv) 2 ∈ (4 ∪ 5 ∪ 6 ∪ 7), that is, the union of regions 4, 5, 6, and 7 does not contain region 2;

(v)   (3 ∪ 7) ∈ (1 ∪ 2 ∪ 4 ∪ 5), that is, the union of regions 1, 2, 4, and 5 does not contain the union of regions 3 and 7.

Now, let's superimpose the diagram for the SMP system onto the diagram for the 8 system (Figure 2.5) in order to compare the two. First of all, notice that the two systems are distinct descriptions of the relationships between the regions. Given that region S in the SMP system corresponds to region (1 ∪ 2 ∪ 4 ∪ 5) in the 8 system, the statement "S is primitive" is true in the SMP system, but "(1 ∪ 2 ∪ 4 ∪ 5) is primitive" is false in the 8 system. However, the two descriptions are extensionally isomorphic; they are two different ways of describing the same set of relations between regions that preserve the overall structural features and relations, and in that sense they deal with the same "facts." Indeed, a comparison of facts (i) to (v) of the SMP and 8 systems will reveal that they are system-relative descriptions expressing the same relationship. Compare, for example, item (i) in the respective systems: "(S ∩ [M ∩ P]) ⊂ S" and "5 ⊂ (1 ∪ 2 ∪ 4 ∪ 5)." The former states the fact that the intersection of the SMP system

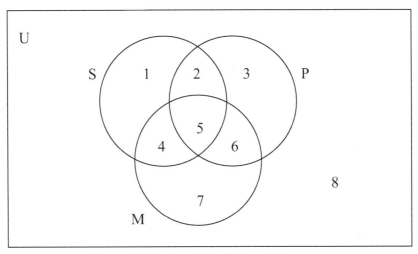

Figure 2.5. Overlay of the SMP- and 8-systems

primitives is contained by one of the primitives, but the former says that one of the 8 system primitives is contained by the union of four primitives. So, which system correctly captures the relationships between the regions on the Venn diagram? Either will do equally well—and the question that becomes utterly moot is "Which regions are *really* the primitive ones?" The point is that the fundamental ontology is relative to some system or other.

So, in Goodman's (1978) view, the theories of light as a wave and as a particle are two actual, equally privileged versions of electromagnetic radiation, even though they are ontologically disjoint; there are photons according to the latter, but not according to the former. Likewise, Zermelo, von Neumann, and I give three ontologically diverse yet equally privileged, isomorphic models of the natural numbers. Importantly, Goodman does not believe that all descriptions of the world are true or right:

> Willingness to accept countless alternative true or right world-versions does not mean that everything goes, that tall stories are as good as short ones, that truths are no longer distinguished from falsehoods, but only that truth must be otherwise conceived than as correspondence with a ready-made world. Though we make worlds by making versions, we no more make a world by putting symbols together than a carpenter makes a chair by putting pieces of wood together at random. The multiple worlds I countenance are just the actual worlds made by and answering to true or right

versions. Worlds possible or impossible supposedly answering to
false versions have no place in my philosophy. (94)

Observe that the Lowenheim-Skolem theorem implies that there are non-
standard models of first-order number theory, but none of these can be a
true model of the numbers we know and love; and I assume, as well, that
some ancient Greek versions of light are illusory, wrong, or dubious. What
we need, then, is Goodman's account of the distinction between true statements, theories, models, or versions and those that are false, empty, illusory,
or dubious. This is critical to our project of finding the philosophical value
in an American Indian worldview, for true versions create well-made worlds,
while false or empty versions create "ill-made" or "unmade" worlds, and
we have seen that since first contact with American Indians the Western
intellectual tradition has almost always regarded the Native worldview as
primitive and uncivilized, false and empty.

True Versions and Well-Made Worlds

We have seen that truth cannot be a correspondence between statements,
theories, models, or versions and a ready-made world of facts. Facts are fabricated; objects and kinds are relative to a particular linguistically informed
frame of reference. So, then, what makes it true that "There were three
cardinals around my feeder" but false that "The cardinal atop the feeder
redded"? Why is it true that "All emeralds are green," but false that "All
emeralds are grue"? What, in Goodman's view, makes a statement, theory,
model, or version true?

Note that an answer to the question, "What makes a statement true?"
works as well for "What makes a theory, model, or version true?" because
Goodman (1978) collapses the distinction between individual statements of
fact and the overall theories that fabricate them and in which they are, in
turn, embedded. "Facts," he says, "are theory-laden; they are as theory-laden
as we hope our theories are fact-laden. Or in other words, facts are small
theories, and true theories are big facts" (96–97).

In the absence of correspondence, coherence is the natural candidate
for a criterion of truth. However, as Goodman correctly argues, coherence
may be necessary for a true version, but it is hardly sufficient for truth.
A statement of the form "p & q" is logically consistent with a statement
of the form "p v q"; both can be true for some distribution of truth values for the components. Consider, however, that although the disjunction
"Either light is a particle or light is a wave" is true in the particle theory
of light, the statement "Light is a particle and light is a wave" is not.

Indeed, the latter would be rather unwelcome. Anyway, J. R. R. Tolkien's world of Middle-earth—filled with hobbits, elves, and wizards—is certainly internally coherent, but we do not regard it as a true version constructing a well-made actual world. While coherence might be necessary for truth, it is not sufficient. Then what is?

As a first approximation, Goodman (1978) suggests that "a version is taken to be true when it offends no unyielding beliefs and none of its own precepts," where unyielding beliefs are exemplified by, among other things, "long-lived reflections of laws of logic, short-lived reflections of recent observations, and other convictions and prejudices ingrained with varying degrees of firmness," and precepts are exemplified by "choices among alternate frames of reference, weightings, and derivational bases" (17). These kinds of versions exhibit a kind of rightness that is closely related but different from truth—acceptability—and *ultimate* acceptability "serves as a sufficient condition for truth" (Goodman 1984: 38).

Clearly, the notion of the ultimate acceptability of a statement, theory, model, or version demands further discussion. First, Goodman (1984) makes clear that he is not offering a *definition* of truth as ultimate acceptability, "for we take truth to be constant while acceptability is transient. Even what is maximally acceptable at one moment may become inacceptable [*sic*] later" (38). However, ultimate acceptability—even if we can never be quite sure we've achieved it—is "as steadfast as truth."

In order for a statement, theory, model, or version to be acceptable—to be a *right rendering*—it must satisfy a number of conditions; indeed, although acceptability and truth are distinct, we sometimes even regard the satisfaction of these conditions as tests for truth. Now, these tests do not all carry equal weight when determining a right rendering; a version may satisfy one condition only tenuously, but it is still acceptable because it passes other tests. However, the violation of some important conditions is unacceptable.

"Among the most explicit and clear-cut standards of rightness we have anywhere," asserts Goodman (1978), "are those for validity of a deductive argument" (125). If the deductive reasoning employed to conclude a statement is invalid, then the statement is unacceptable. And a version containing both of the contradictory statements "The feeder moved" and "The feeder did not move" would certainly be unacceptable, for in such a version *every other statement must be true*. Of course, this standard of rightness is closely related to truth, for valid inferences are truth-preserving, and sound arguments—valid arguments with true premises—guarantee the truth of their conclusions.

A second important standard of rightness is strong induction: If the inductive reasoning employed to conclude a statement is weak, then the statement is unacceptable. Unlike valid deduction, however, a strong inductive inference can have a false conclusion even with true premises. "What, then," Goodman (1984) asks, "is required for inductive [strength]?" (37). Besides certain formal relations between premises and conclusions, *right categorization* is required. Recall that not all ways the world can be sorted into kinds—categorized—have a useful or familiar place in a world version; the kind created by Goodman's "grue" again nicely serves to illustrate. Although "green" is projectible, and past observations confirm the general hypothesis that all emeralds are green, "grue" is not projectible, so concluding that all emeralds are grue based on past observations is inductively weak—hence unacceptable. Again, the difference is that because of a long history of past inductive successes, "green" is weighted more heavily than "grue"; the former is better entrenched, and so is a relevant kind, whereas the latter is not. The extension of "green" is a right categorization; the extension of "grue" is not. It bears repeating that there are many ways to categorize the world, but right categorization is dependent on past inductive success *within* a linguistic tradition. "All emeralds are green" is acceptable in our linguistic tradition, whereas "skypaki-" applies to emeralds in the Shawnee tradition because an emerald "either greens or blues."

The utility of a statement, theory, model, or version is a third standard of rightness, although on its own clearly not a test for truth; indeed, nothing is more useful in the physics of breadbox-sized objects than the fictional frictionless plane—but I wouldn't go looking for one at Home Depot. And while not embracing Goodman's constructivist view, Nancy Cartwright (1983) argues that the fundamental laws of physics, like the universal law of gravitation, are embraced for their explanatory power—a feature of utility—but their simplistic and unqualified formulations are false; they do not truly describe how bodies behave. Qualifying them to reflect what we truly observe, she argues, results in laws that are not very useful, for they have been robbed of explanatory power. Consider that *only in a vacuum*—a quite unnatural condition—will objects fall at a uniform acceleration independent of weight.[7]

These considerations suggest a fourth standard of rightness for versions, namely, simplicity. Given two versions, the simpler one—the one that posits fewer primitive objects, relations, and complex processes—is more acceptable. Indeed, it was simplicity that first gave the Copernican model of planetary motion a toehold in competition with its deeply entrenched Ptolemaic rival. I should note that Goodman (1972) holds simplicity in high regard as a test for truth:

> My insistence that simplicity is of the essence of science has sometimes been misinterpreted as the claim that simplicity is

the only or the always-overriding factor in the choice of basis. Obviously, considerations such as brevity, clarity, convenience, familiarity, and utility for a special purpose usually enter also . . . but these other factors, unlike simplicity and truth, are minor aids rather than major aims. A scientific system may be cumbersome, difficult, strange; but with no simplicity we have no system and no science at all. (277)

Finally, we may infer from Goodman's discussion that there is another important standard for the rightness of versions: If a version is *empty*, then the version is unacceptable. By now we're used to the idea that facts are fabricated, that there were cardinals about the feeder—and neither cardinal nor short cardinal temporal slices—because of the objectifying and categorizing devices of language. And, given the fundamental beliefs and precepts grounding our everyday view of the world, the statement "The cardinals were red" is true, whereas the statement "The cardinals redded" is false. But while the former is fact and the latter fiction, each is consistent with the content of our sense experiences. Indeed, the perceptual content of "The cardinals were red" and "The cardinals redded" is *identical*. The two facts are distinguished by the way that the perceptual content is organized into linguistically constructed conceptual categories. Without the conceptual devices of a language, experience is formless and facts indiscernible. "[P]erception without conception is *blind*" (Goodman 1978: 6).

Thus, the unstructured content of sense experience can no more be a world version than a rowdy gathering without rules of order can be a meeting. On the other hand, could we have a meeting with the rules of order in place, but without the gathering? Clearly not—the meeting hall would be *empty*. Likewise, a statement, theory, model, or version is *empty* when there is no perceptual content to be identified, categorized, and organized by language. "[C]onception without perception is merely *empty*. . . . Predicates, pictures, other labels, schemata, survive want of application. . . . We can have words without a world" (6). No wonder Goodman (1983) declares as "inacceptable [*sic*] without explanation . . . powers or dispositions, counterfactual assertions, entities or experiences that are possible but not actual, neutrinos, angels, devils, and classes"—all notoriously imperceptible, and so empty notions (33). "Non-actual possibilia," "Platonic forms," "angels," and "devils" are labels that survive despite having no perceptual content. They label nothing.[8]

We have discussed a few standards for the acceptability of versions—standards of rightness—but our consideration is certainly not exhaustive. Versions offending against our linguistically informed ontological beliefs about enduring physical objects or the general veracity of our own senses must be ruled as unacceptable as those that violate the laws of logic or project unprojectible predicates. Of course, minds change about even the most deeply held beliefs and precepts, as when Galileo challenged the Aristotelian truth—and common sense—that, given two objects of unequal weight, the heavier one will fall faster. The important point here is that statements, models, theories, or versions will be unacceptable if they conflict with deeply entrenched beliefs, accepted precepts, habits of mind, and the evidence of perception.[9] Acceptable versions aspire to truth and those that are ultimately acceptable are true. And true versions are valuable, for true versions construct well-made worlds.

Nonlinguistic Versions and the Advancement of Understanding

Thus far, we have been concerned exclusively with linguistic, literal versions of the world—statements, theories, and models. However, Goodman (1978) and Goodman and Elgin (1988) famously argue that the world versions crafted in the arts also contribute to the making of an actual world. Indeed, one of the major themes of his *Ways of Worldmaking* is that "the arts must be taken no less seriously than the sciences as modes of discovery, creation, and enlargement of knowledge in the broad sense of advancement of the understanding" (102). In the case of fiction, a version may be literally false, but metaphorically true. " 'Don Quixote,' taken literally, applies to no one, but taken figuratively, applies to many of us . . . [The] application of the fictive term 'Don Quixote' to actual people . . . effects a reorganization of our familiar world by picking out and underlining as a relevant kind a category that cuts across well-worn ruts" (103–104).

However, nonlinguistic and nondenotational art forms relying on exemplification and expression are no less important in the making of an actual world. Music, painting, poetry—and the dance—serve to reorganize, sometimes reaffirm, and often broaden the boundaries of the world. Goodman argues that these symbol systems affect some of the same sorts of new discriminations and integrations as literal verbal systems, combining, dividing, and creating new relevant kinds. And, unsurprisingly, Goodman (1978) finds that the artist and the scientist employ similar world-building and rebuilding processes, although their products and performances are unlike.

The most notable consequence of blurring the once sharp distinction between science and art is the diminishing importance of knowledge construed as *justified true belief*—and the corresponding onerous epistemic task of collecting as many true beliefs as possible. (How many have you?) Instead, as Goodman (1978) observes, "knowing or understanding is seen as ranging beyond the acquiring of true beliefs to the discovering and devising of fit of all sorts," ranging from the fit of a true statement within a descriptive world version to the fit of a painting within a movement, a musical composition within a style, or a dance performance within its choreography. And the successful discovering and devising of these various kinds of fits of versions with other versions, whether literal or nonliteral, verbal or nonverbal, denotational or nondenotational—as well as the construction of well-made worlds by those "right renderings"—ultimately depends on the rightness of categorization, "a matter of fit with practice" (138).

It should be obvious from my largely uncritical rehearsal of Goodman's constructivism that I find much to applaud in his account. First, to my mind the speciousness of the bare fact as an epistemological foundation for knowledge of the world is well established, and I agree with Goodman that we construct facts about the world, both linguistically and nonlinguistically. Second, I hold that there is a multiplicity of ontologically diverse, yet equally privileged constructed worlds; indeed, all of the diverse ways that sense experiences could be objectified and categorized into objects and kinds, and all of the different sorts of predicates that could be projected across space and time boggle the mind. Third, because there are no bare facts, truth must be reconceived as something other than the correspondence of statements, theories, models, or version to facts that are independent of some description or other, and Goodman's view that ultimate acceptability is a sufficient condition for truth—if not the functional equivalent of truth—seems quite plausible. Finally, I find the world-making power of nonlinguistic systems—including dance—and the resulting collapse of the distinction between art and science to be particularly attractive. All that said, Goodman and I have some pretty serious disagreements, which are the focus of the next chapter.

3

True Versions and Cultural Bias

This chapter begins the argument for the legitimacy of an American Indian world version from a constructivist perspective. It begins with a critique of Goodman's view, in which I gently suggest that his constructive nominalism cannot be the whole story, because mental acts of world construction are *real*, *members of kinds*, and *necessarily antecedent* to the actual worlds constructed; hence my view, which I call *constructive realism*. I argue that because Goodman's criteria for the ultimate acceptability of a world version are culturally biased, they beg the question of acceptability against any non-Western world version, especially a Native world version. Finally, I argue that a culturally sophisticated reinterpretation of Goodman's criteria should find an American Indian world version ultimately acceptable, hence numbered among the internally consistent, equally privileged, well-made actual worlds.

Constructive Realism:
Variations on a Theme by Goodman

My very first philosophy professor, Bernard McCormick, made this argument about radical relativist views that still resonates: It cannot be the case that everything is relative, for the absoluteness of the claim is self-refuting. Either the claim "everything is relative" is itself relative, thus opening the door to absolutes, or "everything is relative" is itself an absolute, so the claim is false. Now, it is unclear to me how Goodman's radical relativism can escape this sort of self-referential paradox, for his view is expressed in language, and so like every other statement, theory, model, or version, its objects and kinds—and its facts—are fabricated by language. But the relevant kinds in Goodman's constructivist theory include the very kinds of world-constructing processes—among them composition, decomposition, weighting, and ordering—used to make all world versions, including his own. So, if all relevant kinds are fabrications within a particular version, *then Goodman cannot give a general account of "ways of world making"!* Meta-phorically speaking, he cannot see beyond the bounds of his own particular version because he cannot give an account that applies to all versions. Goodman might reply, "well, so much the better," as Nietzsche (1989: 31–33) did when answering a similar criticism, but I believe there is a more satisfying response.

Goodman argues for an ontological pluralism, that there is a multiplic-ity of actual, equally privileged world versions, where we are to understand true world versions as extensionally isomorphic to an ultimately acceptable version. Remember, however, that world versions do not materialize out of thin air; they are constructed using the materials from other world versions. Over time, theories and models are refinements of or reactions against their predecessors. But in another more important sense these symbol systems must arise from something else—something that is not a mere antecedent symbol system. Statements, theories, models, and the entire world versions that contain them are *products* of our acts of construction—our composings and decomposings, weightings and orderings, among them. And, I maintain, there simply could not be the succession or multiplicity of world versions Goodman embraces without the various kinds of acts of construction that produce them. To deny this would be, by analogy, to deny that the acts of carpenters are necessary to transform the raw materials of boards and nails into a house. Houses are constructed from other materials, just as world versions are constructed from other world versions—*but someone must engage in the acts of constructing.*[1]

Now, the acts of carpentry—hammering, sawing, and so forth—are independent of any particular house. And just as many different wooden structures can be built using a single set of tools, the many equally privileged worlds are constructed using a common set of world-constructing processes, like composings, weightings, and orderings. A multiplicity of worlds does not imply a multiplicity of *ways* of constructing those worlds. Moreover, it seems to me that we cannot give a *general* theory of how a multiplicity of actual worlds is constructed—a theory that applies to all versions *without the perils of self-reference*—unless world-constructing acts are understood as being members of kinds that are independent of any and all particular versions. A rough, but yet helpful way to think about what I am proposing—a view I call *constructive realism*—is this: Whenever the nominalist Goodman talks about a kind of world version constructing process—composition, decompo-sition, weighting, ordering, and so on—I understand them *not* as fabricated kinds—as mere extensions of a predicate weighted within Goodman's par-ticular version—but as genuine, realistically construed kinds of constructing processes that are logically and ontologically prior to and independent of the multiple actual world versions their exemplars produce.

I have argued for such a view (Norton-Smith 1991, 2001) in the rather narrow context of arithmetic. Beginning with Philip Kitcher's (1984) astute insight that rudimentary arithmetical truths are true in virtue of collecting and combining activities, and in view of the limitations of his "Mill arithmetic," I developed a view of number as a property of kinds of human activity called collective kinds[2] (Norton-Smith 1992). I have come to regard collecting as a world version constructing process on a par with Goodman's other objectifying and categorizing processes. In fact, his account of how the world is organized into kinds is quite close to my account of collecting.

Consider again my backyard scene, focusing now on the woodpile under the eastern gray (Figure 3.1). We have already seen how the statement "There are three sticks of wood" is the fabrication of a fact through the devices of a language. But let's take a closer look at how we construct the fact. First, as Goodman teaches, we identify the sticks as individual objects—and not as temporal stick slices, stick mass, and the like—after which we collect them. Now, to say that *I collect the sticks of firewood* is to say that *I represent or view the sticks as a collection*. Collecting does not produce an independently existing physical entity—a collection—because such an odd physical entity would be perceptually indistinguishable from its uncollected components; a physical collection of sticks of firewood would be indistinguishable from the uncollected sticks. Instead, a collection is a product of an organizing of experience, just as Goodman argues. When we collect we represent to ourselves that the objects collected are connected

Figure 3.1. An eastern gray on the woodpile

or associated, as when I earlier collected Beethoven's "Choral Fantasy" and the number 42. And just as the specification of a predicate plays a central role in the fabrication of kinds, so the specification of a predicate is a very useful way to collect (Norton-Smith 1991). I use the predicate "grammatical mark on this page" to represent the individual grammatical marks on the page as a collection—*with a cardinality*. Likewise, "stick of wood under the eastern gray" collects the individual objects, that is, I regard the objects as a collection that has the cardinality three. So, "There are three sticks of wood" is a fact about how I have organized the world.

Importantly, in viewing my backyard scene, a native Ojibwa speaker would organize the world in a different way—seeing a *different* fact—saying "niswi-aatig-misan"—roughly translated as "three-one-dimensional-rigid sticks of firewood," with the count word "niswi-aatig" meaning "three-one-dimensional-rigid" and the stem "misan" meaning "sticks of firewood." Notice that the morpheme "-aatig"—meaning "one-dimensional-rigid"—is incorporated into the structure of the count word itself. This is just one of a group of numerical suffixes, identified by J. Peter Denny (Closs 1986), that are used to classify important properties of objects used in traditional Ojibwa life. Other classifiers include "-aabik" as in "midaasw-aabik-asiniin" (ten-hard stones) and "-minag" as in "niizho-minag-miinan" (two-three-dimensional blueberries). The crucial point to observe is that Ojibwa speakers—and probably speakers of all Algonquin languages—organize the numerical world in a different way than we do. Although our count word "two" applies to collections of stones or roots or bears, Ojibwa speakers employ three distinct count words with these collections, organizing the world in three distinct ways: "*niizho-aabik*-asiniin" means "*two-hard* stones," "*niizho-aabiig*-miinan" means "*two-one-dimensional-flexible* roots," and "*niizh*-makoog" means "*two* bears."

From these and like comparisons I have argued (Norton-Smith 2004) that indigenous numerical thought is genuinely different from that found in the Western tradition. For example, in Shawnee and Ojibwa languages the number words are particles most often functioning as adjectives modifying nouns referring to collections of objects—and not as nouns—suggesting a commitment to numerical properties but not to numbers as objects (Norton-Smith 2004). Using Goodman's terminology, we might say that the speakers of these languages construct genuinely different numerical versions of the world. And yet, however different Native numerical world versions are from their Western counterparts, it remains the case that collecting acts—acts of viewing objects as collections, that is, as entities with a cardinality—is the logically necessary antecedent to counting and to the rudimentary arithmetical facts about collecting and combining activities in each tradition. And if we are going to give a general theory of world version constructing processes that applies both to Western and non-Western traditions, then the action kind *collecting* must be something more than the mere extension of the predicate "collecting" in a particular Western philosophical account. Thus follows my view that we are *not* to understand the kinds of world-making processes Goodman so well describes—composing and decomposing, weighting and ordering, projecting and collecting—as a nominalist would, but as a *metaphysical realist* does.

I anticipate the obvious objection that I am giving an account of how some part of the world *really* is, but in describing it I am imposing an order, "for the talk imposes structure, conceptualizes, ascribes properties" (Goodman 1978: 6). However, this is not just another version of the world on a par with other versions or descriptions—like the naïve realist's or NASA's versions of my backyard scene. Not unlike Kant's project, I am giving a meta-theoretical account—a meta-version, if you will—of the kinds of constructive processes necessary to organize and structure *any* world whatsoever. Otherwise, nothing said here applies beyond the bounds of this particular version; and while I know how my house was constructed, how the one next door came to be is a real mystery.

True Versions and Cultural Bias

We have noted Goodman's "willingness to accept countless alternative true or right world versions" as well as his unwillingness to accept just any world version. "The multiple worlds I countenance are just the actual worlds made by and answering to true or right versions. Worlds possible or impossible supposedly answering to false versions have no place in my philosophy" (Goodman 1978: 94). True versions construct well-made worlds, whereas false or empty versions yield "ill-made," "unmade," or "impossible" worlds—like Goodman's dismissive example of a Native story about the earth resting on the back of a tortoise.

We saw in the last chapter that that true versions are ones that are extensionally isomorphic to an ultimately acceptable version, where ultimate acceptability is not identified with truth, but serves as a sufficient condition for truth. Extensionally isomorphic versions may be ontologically diverse, but their overall global structures are preserved. Finally, criteria for the acceptability of a version include deductive validity and inductive rightness, utility, simplicity and nonemptiness (i.e., having a basis in sense experience). However, these criteria for the acceptability of a statement, theory, model, or version are largely culturally determined, and so, then, is the ultimate acceptability of a version. Because Goodman uses his culturally informed criteria for acceptability to distinguish between true versions and those that are false or empty—thus distinguishing well-made from ill-made worlds—his constructivist account is biased against Native versions and worlds in particular, and against any non-Western version and world in general.

Consider first valid deduction, "[a]mong the most explicit and clear cut standards of rightness we have anywhere" (Goodman 1978: 125). Of course, the system in which deductive validity is defined is classical two-valued semantics—a decidedly Western conception of logic. It matters little that Goodman's variant—the calculus of individuals—avoids commitment to classes, for it still assumes the laws of noncontradiction and the excluded middle, and it preserves theorems of its platonistic counterpart. The problem is that Goodman's marriage to a variant of classical logic as a criterion of acceptability begs the question against other nonstandard logics—nonstandard by Western lights, that is—even other logics developed and advanced within the Western tradition. Arguably, a constructivist like Goodman should be more sympathetic to intuitionist or constructivist logics—logics that deny the law of the excluded middle—as developed by L. E. J. Brouwer and Arend Heyting (T. Smith 1981). More to our point, valid deduction within classical two-valued semantics as a criterion for acceptability of a version biases Goodman's account against Native versions and worlds.

Anne Waters (2004a) argues that indigenous thought—and so indigenous ontology, the world of Native people—is framed by a decidedly different logic, which has perpetuated misunderstandings "of precolonial ontology, rationality, beliefs, customs, and institutions of people indigenous to the Americas" (98). Analyzing classical two-valued semantics as "a discrete binary dualist logic," wherein the laws of the excluded middle and noncontradiction hold, Waters draws a comparison between this standard Western conception and the nondiscrete complementary dualist logics embodied by indigenous thought. In such logics, dualisms may emerge (e.g., male–female, good–evil, animate–inanimate) but, being nonbinary, these dualisms are not regarded as opposites. It is not the case that for any proposition p, either p is true or not-p is true, but not both; it is not the case that for any object o and any property p, either o is p or o is non-p, but not both. Moreover, in such logics where dualisms are complementary, it may be the case that something is both p and not-p at the same time in the same sense, without one excluding the other; something may be both good and evil at the same time without the good excluding the evil (Waters 2004a: 97–99). A logical sense that denies the two fundamental tenets of Western logic—noncontradiction and the excluded middle—would clearly be unacceptable by Goodman's lights; but then, only versions assuming classical two-valued semantics and its isomorphic variants—should we say, *standard Western logics*—satisfy his criterion of valid deduction for acceptability.

Waters explores one significant consequence of this difference in the underlying logical commitments, namely, the different constructions of gender in the Western and Native traditions. She argues that the Western discrete binary logical system grounds the construction of "a discretely gendered person"—one who is either male or female, but not both—period. Not so, Waters (2004a) argues, for Native traditions, because:

> Many Indigenous gender categories are ontologically without fixed boundary. They are animate, nondiscrete, and grounded in a nondiscrete and thus nonbinary dualist ontology. That is, the ontology, as animate (continuously alterable), will be inclusive (nonbinary) rather than exclusive (discrete binary), and have nondiscrete (unbounded) entities rather than discrete (discretely bounded) entities. (107)

As a result, gender categories are constructed as active and complex, diverse and not sharply delineated in indigenous traditions; indeed, Waters asserts that understanding Native constructions of gender may require identifying "diversely intertwined active gender ontologies (multigender ontologies)" (108).

Goodman's culturally informed criterion of inductive rightness is no less biased against Native processes of projection. To see how, it is useful to recall the requirements for a "right" inductive argument. First, true premises are required. Second, all genuine evidence must be available in a right inductive argument; all confirming instances must be available and no negative instances can be omitted. Third, the evidence statements and hypothesis must be expressed in terms of genuine or natural kinds, that is, in terms of projectible predicates like "green," but not "grue." But this requires the right categorization of experience—like organizing experience into the relevant kind green and ignoring the irrelevant kind grue. Finally, right categorization—and the right projection based on it—is primarily a matter of habit; and when equally well-qualified hypotheses conflict, the hypothesis expressed in terms of the better-entrenched predicates carries the day. Importantly, inductively right categories "tend to coincide with categories that are right for science in general" (Goodman 1978: 126–28). That would be, of course, right for Western science.

Now, I argue that Native processes of projection are more cautious, hence different, from those advanced by Goodman in his culturally informed account of a right inductive inference, so his account is biased against the notion that an Indian world version could be true and construct an actual world. I begin with Vine Deloria's comparison of a classic example of Western reasoning and a similar inference expressed as a Native would. His reflections, I argue, reveal a difference in the way that predicates are projected:

> In the West we would submit the following propositional thinking as capable of giving us knowledge: "Socrates is a man; all

men are mortal; Socrates is mortal." For the Indian the response
would be: "Oh, yes, I once met Socrates, and he was just like
the rest of us so I assume he is mortal also." In both cases there
is an assumption. In the proposition "all men are mortal,"-we
cannot truly verify our statement. We have not yet met all men
and we infer from the limited number we have observed that our
statement holds true. The Indian also assumes that all men are
mortal but he requires empirical verification in the remembrance
that Socrates is because he once met Socrates and verified that
he was a man like himself. This process of verification reduces
substantially the number and kinds of statements that Indians
would be willing to make. But it substantially enhances the veracity of statements that are made. Whereas the Western syllogism
simply introduces a doctrine using general concepts and depends
on faith in the chain of reasoning for its verification, the Indian
statement would stand by itself without faith and belief. I suggest that the question of all men's mortality is still open for the
American Indian on the possibility that some men are immortal
but have not yet been encountered. (Deloria 2004: 6)

I interpret Deloria's comparison as making a crucial point about how
predicates are projected in Western and Native worldviews, a point that
reveals a deeper ontological belief about their respective world constructs.
Despite his accurate observation that "[w]e have not yet met all men and
we infer from the limited number we have observed that our statement
holds true," Western inductive reasoners project natural kinds with great
confidence, especially when based on an exquisitely well-established regularity; what Western inductive reasoner would *seriously* doubt that all men are
mortal, all emeralds are green, or that open flames burn uncovered skin?
(Those who do would be regarded as mere quibblers.) However, according to
Deloria, "the question of all men's mortality is still open for the American
Indian on the possibility that some men are immortal but have not yet been
encountered" (6). That is, Native inductive reasoners are more cautious
about projecting natural kinds like "men" and "mortality," and the possibility
of a nonmortal man is a real possibility. So, one cannot accept it on faith
that Socrates is mortal and a man like I am; one must verify.

Does such a mistrust of the more liberal Western process of projecting
predicates evidence that there is something wrong with—perhaps "primitive" about—Native inductive reasonings? Not a bit; in fact, the medieval
scholars who concluded that "all swans are white" should take a lesson.
Rather, Native care in drawing inductive conclusions without constant,
personal verification reveals a deep ontological belief about the nature

of the constructed world, the nature of verification and relatedness as a world-ordering principle. This discussion deserves just a word about Native ontological beliefs, for an extensive consideration of the Native constructed world and relatedness follows in subsequent chapters.

Whether adopting the frame of my backyard feeder or NASA's frame, the underlying Western ontological assumption about the physical world is that it is material and inanimate, mechanical and rational, amenable to quantitative description and governed by fixed physical laws. It is orderly, fixed, and finished. No wonder the natural assumption—expressed by the principle of induction—is that a very well-established regularity will extend into unobserved regions of space and time. All emeralds are green, and all men are mortal. However, the Native version constructs a world that is creative and animate, dynamic and purposeful, interconnected and orderly (but only with the constant intervention of its denizens to help maintain equilibrium), unfixed and unfinished. Indeed, according to Native philosopher of science Gregory Cajete (2004), human beings participate in the creation of an unfinished, living world whose ordering principle is creativity:

> Our universe is still unfolding and human beings are active and creative participants. Creativity is both the universe's ordering principle and its process, part of the greater flow of creativity in nature. It flows from the "implicate order" or inherent potential of the universe, and whatever it produces becomes a part of the "explicate order" of material or energetic expressions. These expressions range from entire galaxies to the quarks and leptons of the subatomic world. Human creativity is located in this immense continuum. (47)

Because the constructed world is animate, creative, and constantly unfolding, it would be somewhat reckless to extend even the most well-verified regularity—to project the most well-entrenched predicate—into the future with unflinching confidence (as would a Western inductive reasoner) without constant verification. Every man I have met has been mortal, so I assume Socrates is, because I have verified that he is like every other man I have met. However, the living world is not fixed—it is still in the process of creation—so the emergence of a nonmortal man or a non-green emerald can never be lightly dismissed. In fact, predictions made in an animate world are only as reliable as predictions made about the behavior of any creative, living being. "[The] idea that everything in the universe is alive, and that the universe itself is alive, is knowledge as useful as anything that Western science has discovered or hypothesized. . . . There are, however, substantial differences in the manner in which predictions are made.

Because the universe is alive, there is choice for all things and the future is always indeterminate"[3] (Deloria 1999: 50).

The American Indian world version also informs how experience is categorized, how experience is organized into relevant kinds. Because entities in the Native constructed world are alive, and especially because they are interconnected, the process of right categorization is ongoing and evolving. This is in keeping with Goodman's (1978) observation that when organizing experience "there must be leeway for progress, for the introduction of novel organizations that make, or take account of, newly important connections and distinctions," that is, no right categorization can be absolutely static (128). However, unlike their Western counterparts, Native constructors of an interconnected and interdependent world actively search for the newly emergent, previously overlooked, unexpected, and strikingly unusual connections between experiences. The panoply of relevant kinds constantly evolves because of the ontological conviction that "we are all relatives":

> "We are all relatives" when taken as a methodological tool for obtaining knowledge means that we observe the natural world by looking for relationships between various things in it. That is to say, everything in the natural world has relationships with every other thing and the total set of relationships makes up the natural world as we experience it. (Deloria 1999: 34)

Because Native observers of the world actively search for relationships in organizing experience—that is, employ relatedness as a world-ordering principle—connections between apparently disparate experiences by Western lights are recognized as relevant and employed for practical purposes. Deloria (1999) tells a story about one such connection, recognized by the Pawnee, between the maturing of the seed pods of the milkweed during the late summer hunt on the high plains and the immanent maturing of the corn crop in their villages some distance away.

> In fact, the Pawnee had been able to discern, through observation or by information given to them in a ceremony, that corn and milkweed had about the same growing season. To be more precise, milkweed was a bit faster growing than corn because it would take several weeks to return to their villages after having examined the milkweed. (35)

According to Deloria, the Pawnee had perceived a plant relationship, using the milkweed as an indicator plant so they could tell how the corn crop was progressing. We would say that in the Pawnee world version there was a useful relationship constructed between milkweed and corn-maturing experiences.[4]

Finally, recall that Goodman holds that right categorization—and the right projection based on it—is principally habitual, and that the degree to which a predicate is entrenched is telling in competitions between conflicting hypotheses. Certainly, the entrenchment of kinds and relations is important, especially in a tradition that holds the wisdom of the elders in such high regard. However, given that the Indian world is animate, creative, and constantly unfolding, one cannot be dogmatic about the boundaries, membership, or duration of a kind or relation. "The world of nature is in constant flux; therefore, Native science does not attempt to categorize firmly within the domains of ideas, concepts, or laws" (Cajete 2004: 55). So, the entrenchment of a predicate or a relation—albeit grounded in habit—becomes less important as a criterion of their viability or longevity in an American Indian constructed world than Goodman argues.

Utility, as a criterion for the ultimate acceptability of a statement, theory, model, or version is—perhaps surprisingly—no less culturally informed, for within the context of any frame of reference one must ask, "Useful for whom and for what purpose?" The Western tradition, which constructs a natural world that is inert and material, lawlike and mechanical, but a sometimes threatening resource, a very useful version is the one that best enables us to explain and predict, and then conquer, manipulate, and exploit the natural world. Indeed, when considering whether the pragmatists' proposal that truth should be interpreted in terms of utility, Goodman (1978) muses that "[t]he thesis that true statements are those that enable us *to predict or manage or defeat nature* has no little appeal" (122–23; emphasis added). However, we have seen that the American Indian version constructs a world that is animate and dynamic, unfixed and unfinished; human beings participate in the creation of a living world in which everything is interconnected. In such a world where all of our actions and choices are of critical importance—indeed, they contribute to its very *making*—the utility of a world version must be judged far differently than its Western counterpart. "The real interest of the old Indians," Deloria (1999) conveys, "was not to discover the abstract structure of physical reality but rather to find the proper [moral and ethical] road along which, for the duration of a person's life, individuals were supposed to walk" (46). The useful version, then, in a world Deloria terms a *moral universe*, is a normative one. It does not look at the world as an inert natural resource and ask, "How can I predict, manage, or defeat this?" Instead, it sees a living community in which human beings participate and asks, "How should I behave?" So, like the deductive and inductive rightness of world versions, utility as a criterion of ultimate acceptability is culturally determined.

Our "insightful" ethnographer, J. W. Powell, gets this wrong too, as he guffaws at Native childish attempts to explain the "minutia of nature" through American Indian stories. "Their cosmology also deals with all the curious minutia of nature. It explains the tawny patch of fur on the shoulder of the little rabbit, the cardinal head of the woodpecker, the top-knot of the crested jay, and the rattle of the serpent. So there is nothing seen that is not explained" (Powell 1877: 7). What Powell has overlooked is that the purpose of such stories is not to give a Western-styled explanation of the mechanisms of an inert, material world—to expose and convey the facts of how various things in the natural world came to have their characteristic features—but to convey the traditional Native values that we need to walk the right road. Most importantly, the *utility* of the American Indian world version must be understood in this light and with this goal in mind: The useful Native world version is the one that successfully conveys these values through its telling. This is obvious when one considers a traditional Seneca story, "How Buzzard Got His Clothing," which apparently "explains" how all of the birds came to have their characteristic plumage, but whose real goal is to teach a more important *normative* lesson.

As the story goes, the usually shy and humble Buzzard was sent as an emissary to Creator on behalf of the Bird People, for Creator had forgotten to give them clothing when the world was made, and they were cold. Creator made many beautiful feather suits of various sizes and colors, and to Buzzard was given the honor of selecting his own feather suit. One by one, Buzzard examined and rejected the beautiful feather suits, letting them fall to the Earth to the grateful Bird People below. "As beautiful as they are," thought Buzzard, "they are not good enough for the emissary to Creator." But before Buzzard knew it, there was only one suit left—the small, ugly, drab, brown-black suit he now wears. In his embarrassment, Buzzard realized how vain he had been, and he forever blushes, so his head will always be red.[5]

The real normative purpose of the story is obvious to anyone coming to it without a Western prejudice about the function of Native narratives. Buzzard's story is not to be understood as a literal truth, as an explanation of why he has a red head and his feathered suit fits so poorly. It is, instead, a reminder to *us* that we have a particular place in a network of relationships, and to forget that place by pursuing our narrowly individual desires—to lose our humility—ends poorly.

Returning to our consideration of Goodman's criteria for the acceptability of a world version, I offer a brief and pretty disparaging critique of simplicity as a criterion. In short, whether one is a realist or a constructivist about the natural world, there is no nonquestion begging argument that the best version of the world will be the simplest one. Consider first the realist who believes that the true theory or model is the one corresponding to a mind-independent world of facts. Demanding that the ultimately acceptable theory be the simplest one begs the question, because requiring the one true description of the world to be the simplest theory among rivals assumes that the world is simple—but a scientific realist ought to believe that science should discover that the natural world is simple, not assume that it is.

It is actually easier for a constructivist like Goodman to propose simplicity as a criterion of theory choice. For, if one denies truth based on correspondence to a mind-independent world of facts, holding instead that true theories are extensionally isomorphic to an ultimately acceptable theory, and if these theories can be ontologically quite diverse, why not embrace the simplest version, the one that posits the fewest primitive objects and relations? However, the question is begged again, for extensional isomorphism—not simplicity—is the most important characteristic for members of the class of "true" theories, so choosing the simplest from among all of the members of the class reflects more an *aesthetic preference* than a robust criterion of acceptability—"the more elegant theory is the more acceptable." But what could be more culturally informed than one's aesthetic preferences?

Although simplicity is a pseudo-criterion for the acceptability of a world version, nonemptiness is an irrefutable necessary condition. And, unlike deductive validity, inductive rightness, and utility, whether or not a world version is empty—whether or not there is perceptual content to be identified, categorized, and organized by language—is not culturally determined. Indeed, although my constructive realism disagrees with Goodman's nominalism because of the perils of self-reference, and asserts as a fundamental premise that world version constructing processes—composing, decomposing, weighting, ordering, and collecting among them—are genuine natural kinds, it stands firmly with Goodman in asserting a second fundamental premise, namely, that one cannot construct a world without sense experiences to identify and organize. We can—and often do, in Western philosophy—have words without a world. But empty world versions do not construct well-made worlds, so showing that an American Indian world version is not empty— that it is grounded in perception—is essential to this project.

An American Indian Well-Made Actual World

According to Goodman, true versions construct well-made actual worlds, while false or empty versions construct ill-made, unmade, or impossible worlds. The ultimate acceptability of a world version is tantamount to its truth, and statements, theories, models, or versions are ultimately acceptable if they are deductively valid, inductively right, useful, simple, and nonempty. Statements about my backyard feeder—framed by naïve realism and by astrophysics—have served as perfect examples. However, a consequence of Goodman's ontological pluralism is that there are many true, yet onto-logically diverse world versions, namely, the ones that are extensionally isomorphic to an ultimately acceptable version.

I have argued that all of Goodman's criteria for the ultimate accept-ability of a world version—save nonemptiness—are culturally informed or determined. As a result, only Western world versions are ultimately accept-able, hence true, hence construct well-made actual worlds. Non-Western versions based on alternative conceptions of deduction or induction, a dif-ferent sense of utility, or that posit complicated or complex relationships between mind-boggling numbers or kinds of primitive entities are unaccept-able, hence false, hence construct ill-made, unmade, or impossible worlds.

This is an instance of a kind of intellectual arrogance that is not uncommon. Deloria (1999) gives a plausible explanation and a resounding counter:

> Tribal methodologies for gathering information are believed to be "prescientific" in the sense that they are precausal and inca-pable of objective symbolic thought. This belief . . . is a dreadful stereotypical reading of the knowledge of non-Western peoples, and wholly incorrect. (41)

In fact, tribal peoples are as systematic and philosophical as Western scien-tists in their efforts to understand the world around them. They simply use other kinds of data and have goals other than determining the mechanical functioning of things (41). That is, Native world versions are perceived to be primitive, prescientific antecedents to Western scientific versions, and so are rejected out of hand. However, we might interpret Deloria's point to be that tribal people, in fact, have a systematic methodology for identify-ing, categorizing, and organizing experience, but it is different from—not inferior to—a Western methodology. Indeed, Deloria is highlighting the cul-tural differences between Western and non-Western ways of perceiving and understanding the world. I would say, however, that he is highlighting the cultural differences in the ways well-made actual worlds are constructed.

I propose that we reinterpret Goodman's criteria for the ultimate acceptability in a culturally sophisticated way that recognizes their inher-ent bias. In judging whether or not a world version satisfies the criteria for rightness we must ask, "For whom is the world version ultimately accept-able?" As they stand, Goodman's are criteria for ultimate acceptability for a twentieth-century Western analytic philosopher. We can do this by intro-ducing the notion of a cultural frame of reference and indexing the criteria for ultimate acceptability to them. So, when asking after deductive rightness, we determine whether an inference is consistent with the principles of logic adopted within that particular cultural frame of reference. When judging utility, we ask whether a statement, theory, model, or version achieves a purpose or goal informed by a cultural frame. Of course, emptiness will not be culturally determined, so despite such a reinterpretation of the criteria, an empty version constructs an unmade or impossible world. In this culturally sophisticated reinterpretation, a version satisfying these culturally informed criteria will be ultimately acceptable within a cultural frame, hence true, and so will construct a well-made actual world. And within that cultural frame, any version that is extensionally isomorphic to a true version is also true.

Actually, all frames of reference—all world versions—are cultural frames of reference; indeed, all that we have done here is to make explicit the implicit cultural nature of a version. Facts are fabricated, but the fabrication takes place within a linguistically informed tradition; I see a red cardinal atop my feeder, but not a cardinal redding atop the feeder. And what could be more culturally infused and determined than the linguistic frame of reference in which statements, theories, and models are embedded? This, I believe, is related to Deloria's (1999) meaning when, in comparing the American Indian and Western conceptions of reality, he observes that "[r]eality for tribal peoples . . . was the experience of the moment coupled with *the interpretive scheme that had been woven together over the generations*" (38; emphasis added). Donald Fixico (2003) expresses a similar notion, beginning from the premise that one's perceptions are governed by cultural influences:

> From this premise, we can assume that persons of a tribal culture of American Indians perceive subjects differently from those of a non-tribal culture like the American mainstream. Hence, there is a fundamental difference of perception between Indians and white Americans. They understand things differently and accept truth and facts differently. (9)

I suggest that Deloria's "generations-old interpretive scheme" and Fixico's "cultural influences that govern perception" are exactly what I am here calling a *cultural frame of reference*.

In this culturally sophisticated reinterpretation of Goodman's criteria, an American Indian world version is ultimately acceptable within a Native cultural frame of reference. We have visited the nondiscrete complementary dualist logics embodied by indigenous thought, as examined by Waters, and we have explored a Native conception of inductive rightness. More will be discussed about utility and nonemptiness in an American Indian frame in following chapters. (Forget simplicity as a criterion for acceptability; there isn't even a very good reason for including it in Western cultural frame!) In short, if we adopt a culturally sophisticated reinterpretation of Goodman's criteria for the ultimate acceptability of a world version, then an American Indian world will be numbered among the internally consistent, equally privileged, well-made actual worlds, and so it is worthy of philosophical treatment—and respect—from the Western perspective.

4

Relatedness, Native Knowledge, and Ultimate Acceptability

This chapter finishes the argument for the legitimacy of an American Indian world version from a culturally sophisticated constructivist perspective. It also reintroduces and develops *relatedness as a world-ordering principle*—the first common theme in American Indian philosophy. Both come through an examination of a Native conception of knowledge, wherein we consider the notions of truth and verification within the American Indian world version, for these will be important in developing culturally informed criteria for an ultimately acceptable version. And, given that ultimate acceptability is sufficient for truth, and that true versions construct well-made actual worlds, we conclude that an American Indian world is, indeed, numbered among the internally consistent, equally privileged, well-made actual worlds and so it is worthy of philosophical treatment—and respect—from the Western perspective.

Native Knowledge and Relatedness as a World-Ordering Principle

I have proposed a culturally sophisticated reinterpretation of Goodman's criteria for the ultimate acceptability of a world version in which deductive validity, inductive rightness, and utility are judged within a particular cultural frame of reference. Moreover, given such a reinterpretation, an American Indian world will be numbered among the internally consistent, equally privileged, well-made actual worlds—provided, of course, we can establish that the Native world version is not empty, that it is grounded in sense perception.

Deloria's observation that the Native approach to understanding the world differs from a Western methodology in the kinds of experiences that count as evidence and in its ultimate goals suggests that an examination of a Native conception of knowledge will contribute to an exploration of the American Indian world version. Given that truth and processes of verification are critical elements of knowledge, this examination will also help us understand inductive rightness in a Native version, for according to Goodman, truth and the availability of all genuine evidence are important requirements of inductive rightness. Our discussion will have important implications for the culturally informed utility of the Native version and its culturally independent nonemptiness. Finally, a consideration of an American Indian conception of knowledge will reintroduce and develop our first common theme—*relatedness as a world-ordering principle*.

In order to provide a point of comparison—and a point of departure—we begin with an overly simplified review of the most widely embraced Western analysis of knowledge as *justified true belief*. On this analysis—the JTB analysis—three conditions must be met before an individual, S, knows that the proposition *p*. Consider, for example, when Sally knows that there is no greatest prime number. First, Sally must *believe* that there is no greatest prime number. As evidence, consider how silly she would be were Sally to say, "I know there is no greatest prime number, but I don't believe it." Second, it must be *true* that there is no greatest prime number, for one cannot know something false. Indeed, Sally's granny falsely believed that tomatoes are poisonous—being a variety of nightshade—but she could not *know* that tomatoes are poisonous. Finally, Sally's belief must arise from an epistemic process that is in some sense reliable, that is, a process that tends to produce warranted beliefs.[1] For, a Western epistemologist would scoff at the claim that Sally *knows* that there is no greatest prime number if her true belief had arisen, say, from the dream she had last night, when Pythagoras whispered to her that there is no greatest prime number. However, if Sally were to follow and understand the mathematical proof, then by most accounts, her true belief about prime numbers would be justified.

There are a number of things to notice about this brief picture of the Western JTB analysis of knowledge. First of all, notice that the JTB analysis assumes that *propositional* knowledge is the principal, if not the only kind of knowledge worthy of analysis. This kind of knowledge can be characterized as *knowing that p*, where *p* is any purported statement of fact, for example, "Sue knows that the Earth is spherical," "Joe knows that carbon has valence ±4," and "Vine knows that planting corn, beans, and squash together constitutes and completes a natural nitrogen cycle" (Deloria 1999: 12).

Second, the mathematical fact that there is no greatest prime number is a relatively esoteric and eternal bit of information from number theory, one that just happens to have some pretty useful practical implications for, among other enterprises, encoding theory—it guarantees an endless supply of prime numbers for some kinds of encryption codes. This demonstrates that in the Western tradition no proposition is immune from investigation and any statement is a potential candidate for knowledge, whether or not practical results follow. Consider just a few of the obscure and relatively impractical propositions considered by Western philosophers over the years: "Nothing has an intrinsic value," "Each mental event is identical to a physical event," and even "Knowledge is justified true belief." The Western epistemic goal, of course, is to collect as much propositional knowledge—as many justified true beliefs—as possible, without much regard for any practical applications (Burkhart 2004: 21).

Third, notice that however the truth clause of the JTB analysis is fleshed out, as correspondence, coherence, utility, or even as Goodman does (where truth is almost tantamount to ultimate acceptability in a frame of reference), truth is a property of *statements*. So, for example, on the correspondence theory the statement "The Earth is spherical" is true if and only if it corresponds to the mind-independent fact that the Earth is spherical, and on the coherence theory the statement "Carbon has valence ±4" is true if and only if it is consistent with other theory and observation statements within chemical theory.

Finally, the JTB analysis assumes that the individual human subject is the fundamental "unit" of knowing, that a definition of knowledge is properly formulated in terms of conditions met by individual knowers—whether Sally or Sue, Joe or Vine—as opposed to, say, conditions a community must meet in order to know. This is, of course, not at all surprising, because the Western tradition generally regards human beings as essentially individuals in most of its moral, political, and epistemic analyses.

Excellent accounts of an American Indian conception of knowledge can be found in Burkhart (2004), Cheney (2005), Cheney and Hester (2000), Deloria (1999), and Fixico (2003). My consideration owes much to them and I thank them here. I happened upon Hester and Cheney's (2001) elegant reflections on Native epistemology well after my clumsy account could be improved, and I am heartened that our views are "consonant," as Lee Hester kindly put it.

Burkhart frames his presentation of American Indian epistemology with four philosophical principles—better thought of, he reflects, as "ways of being"—the first of which he calls the *principle of relatedness*. Rather than considering relatedness as a realistically construed "way of being"—a way the world is independent of any world version—we will understand relatedness as *a world-ordering principle*, as a way American Indians categorize, organize, and order sense experience.

Remember, the constructivist idea is that *there are no bare facts*, that the pure content of our sense experiences alone underdetermines how the world *really* is, and any one of a number of radically different actual worlds is consistent with experience. Instead, we agree with Goodman that worlds are created by the categorization and ordering of sense experiences through the devices of a language, but also, as we will later see, through other sorts of performances with symbols—prayer, dance, ceremony, and gifting among them. World-constructing processes include composition, decomposition, weighting, and ordering, all of which depend on and help determine how our sense experiences—*and our worlds*—are organized into objects and kinds. As we've seen, *ordering*—creating various patterns in sense experience—is a particularly important world-constructing process, especially for Natives who *actively* search for the newly emergent, previously overlooked, unexpected, and strikingly unusual connections between experiences. *We say that creating patterns of relatedness in sense experience is central to the making of the American Indian world.*

All beings and their actions in the American Indian world are related and interconnected, so knowing about the world involves actively seeking out newly emerging connections between experiences. Reiterating Deloria's (1999) earlier observation, " 'We are all relatives' when taken as a methodological tool for obtaining knowledge means that we observe the natural world by looking for relationships between various things in it" (34). Fixico (2003) expresses the same important notion in his explanation of "seeing," the way traditional American Indians perceive and think about the world:

> "Seeing" is visualizing the connection between two or more entities or beings, and trying to understand the relationship between them within the full context of things identified within a culturally based system. . . . This holistic perception is the indigenous ethos of American Indians and how they understand their environment, the world, and the universe. (2)

It is difficult to underestimate the importance of relatedness in understanding the American Indian world version, for it is reinforced either implicitly or explicitly by most Native stories. Indeed, the construction of a world wherein all entities—all persons, places, and actions—are interconnected will be a recurring theme throughout the remainder of our project. Consider, for example, a Menominee story recorded by Alanson Skinner and John Satterlee (1915):

> Once an Indian had a revelation from the head of all the frogs and toads. In the early spring, when all the frogs and toads thaw out they sing and shout more noisily than at any other time of the year. This Indian made it a practice to listen to the frogs every spring when they first began, as he admired their songs,

and wanted to learn something from them. He would stand near the puddles, marshes, and lakes to hear them better, and once when night came he lay right down to hear them.

In the morning, when he woke up, the frogs spoke to him, saying: "We are not all happy, but in very deep sadness. You seem to like our crying but this is our reason for weeping. In early spring, when we first thaw out and revive we wail for our dead, for lots of us don't wake up from our winter sleep. Now you will cry in your turn as we did!"

Sure enough, the next spring the Indian's wife and children all died, and the Indian died likewise, to pay for his curiosity to hear the multitude of frogs. So this Indian was taught what has been known ever since by all Indians that they must not go on purpose to listen to the cries of frogs in the early spring. (470)

The Indian certainly learned a lesson about the frogs' song, but it was not one he had hoped to steal away without permission. Brought to the songs by a puerile curiosity and a selfish desire to learn something from them, the Indian slept with the frogs, and so shared their sorrow and their fate; the Indian became like a frog—*became brother to the frogs*. If he had remembered that we are all relatives, he would have occurred to him that his and the frogs' lives and actions are interconnected; there is no innocent observation of the world without consequence.

At this point, the Western ethicist recoils, then counters with these arguments: It is unfair to punish the Indian and his family with death, for observing the frogs did them no harm, so observing the frogs was not wrong. Moreover, punishment is unfair, because the Indian intended no harm to the frogs, so he did no wrong. But these arguments—the first consequentialist and the second deontological—are framed within a different moral universe. In the Native world version, everything is related and we are all relatives, so all entities and beings are interconnected, valuable by virtue of those interconnections, and due *respect*. Listening to the frogs to take away something without their permission—to "learn something"—was *disrespectful*; it is not the way one treats one's relatives. Forgetting this responsibility was the fault that fused the Indian's fate to the frogs'.[2]

Returning to our comparison of the Western and Native conceptions of knowledge, note that the former views knowledge as propositional—a *knowing that proposition p*—while American Indian knowledge is principally a procedural knowledge—a *knowing how to p*—where p in this instance is an activity, performance, or procedure, perhaps as elaborate as a storytelling, a healing, or a ritual ceremony, or as simple as observing the world to learn something from it. For example, Nonhelema knows how to plant the Three

Sisters—beans, corn, and squash—and Black Elk knows how to perform the ceremonial Horse Dance (Black Elk 2000: 124–35). It is, as well, knowledge that Burkhart (2004) characterizes as lived or embodied, arising from human action and experience and so is "carr[ied] with us"—unlike propositional knowledge, "which seems to be designed to outlast us, to take on a life of its own, to be something eternal" (20). Importantly, because Native knowledge "is shaped and guided by human actions, endeavors, desires, and goals," since "[it] is what we put to use," an account of this kind of knowledge cannot ignore its *utility* in addressing some practical concern or other (21).

This is not to say, of course, that there is no propositional knowledge—no knowing that *p*—in American Indian traditions; indeed, we would make the same mistake to claim that there is no procedural knowledge—no knowing how to *p*—in the Western tradition. In fact, having a bit of procedural knowledge might be sufficient for having a bit of propositional knowledge, at first blush, perhaps something close to the following:

> For subject, S, her or his purpose or goal *g*, and action or performance *p*, if S knows how to *p* to achieve *g*, then S knows that *p* can be successful in achieving *g*.

On the other hand, having the propositional knowledge is not sufficient for having the procedural knowledge; Sally knows that swimming can be successful in crossing the river, but that does not imply that she knows how to swim across the river.

Stressing the procedural nature of American Indian knowledge emphasizes that it is shaped by human goals and purposes, and it cannot be understood apart from its utility in addressing some practical concern or other. And, in contrast to the Western scientific goal of discovering the laws governing an inert physical universe, the most important concern—the ultimate goal—in a Native effort to understand the world is "to find the proper road along which, for the duration of a person's life, individuals were supposed to walk":

> That is to say, there is a proper way to live in the universe: there is a content to every action, behavior, and belief. The sum total of our life experiences has a reality. There is a direction to the universe, empirically verified in the physical growth cycles of childhood, youth, and old age, with the corresponding responsibility of every entity to enjoy life, fulfill itself, and increase in wisdom and the spiritual development of personality. (Deloria 1999: 46)

You see, there are no inconsequential or morally neutral actions in the American Indian world version, a perspective Burkhart (2004) calls the *moral universe principle*: "The idea is simply that the universe is moral. Facts, truth, meaning, even our existence are normative. In this way, there is no difference between what is true and what is right. On this account, then, all investigation is moral investigation" (17).

This is not, of course, making the silly claim that everything that is the case is also right. *Otherwise, the five-hundred-year history of disease, depredation, and dispossession that Native people have suffered at the hands of colonial powers is right!* Instead, the moral universe principle tells us that everything we do and say—even everything we think—has a moral dimension. Unlike the common Western attitude that there is a sharp distinction between fact and value—where the question "Can I do it?" is utterly distinct from "Should I do it?"—one cannot avoid the moral deliberation before acting nor escape the moral consequences afterward in a moral universe; the curious medical researcher can never simply try to create new stem cell lines—to learn something from them—and ignore the moral implications of or avoid the moral responsibility for her experiments. Like our curious Indian who shared the fate of the frogs, the researcher will bear the consequences of her curiosity, because all investigation is moral investigation.[3]

It is important to stress the *utility* of Native knowledge in addressing some practical concern, and ultimately finding the proper road along which a person should walk, for utility, judged within a particular cultural frame of reference, is one of the criteria for the ultimate acceptability of a world version on our culturally sophisticated reinterpretation of Goodman's constructivism. Indeed, the utility criterion within the American Indian world version differs from its Western counterpart, because Goodman's criterion judges the utility of a statement, theory or model (i.e., propositions) rather than the utility of actions, performances, and procedures. That said, remember that in Goodman's (1978) view all sorts of activities and performances, including those relying on exemplification and expression, are as important in the making of an actual world as propositional systems—hence follows his belief that there is a rather artificial boundary between the world-building processes of the artist and the scientist (107). And, frankly, it would be hard to imagine dismissing utility as a crucial criterion in judging the acceptability of a world version grounded in practical activity, performance, and procedure.

Likewise, I now emphasize the *experiential content* of Native knowledge, again because of our earlier conclusion that little of philosophical value will be found in an empty American Indian world version, that is, in a world version where there is a conceptual categorization—a labeling by predicates, pictures, gestures, and so forth—but no perceptual content to be identified, categorized, and organized. Indeed, we even concluded that the emptiness of a version is sufficient for its unacceptability. After offering the same caution and reminder as in our previous reflections about the utility of Native knowledge, I find it equally unlikely that a world version grounded in action and experience would be devoid of perceptual content. In fact, in his discussion of Native science, Gregory Cajete (2004) stresses the perceptual foundation of knowledge. "In the conceptual framework of philosophy," he writes, "Native American science may be said to be based upon perceptual phenomenology. . . . The central premise of phenomenology roots the entire tree of knowledge in the soil of direct physical and perceptual experience of the earth" (45).

Interestingly enough, we might interpret Burkhart's third American Indian epistemic principle, the *limits of questioning principle*, as securing the Indian world version *against* emptiness. Because Native knowledge is gained from and used in experience, legitimate questions—even those with philosophical content—should arise from some practical problem at hand. The more abstruse questions entertained by Western wonderers—for example, "Is any particular mental event identical to some particular physical event?" or "Is there a greatest prime number?"—fail such a test, for they do not arise from direct experience.[4] According to Burkhart (2004):

> [J]ust because we can imagine something that we would like to know, or can formulate a question regarding, this does not mean that there is, in fact, something to know or that we have formulated an actual question. There is no imagining possible things that might be known. There is only what we actually need to know, and this is a function of our practical lives. A question is, then, real just in case it arises in relation to something directly at hand, some practical concern. (21)

Because both demand an experiential foundation, there is a striking parallel between Burkhart's illegitimate Native questions and Goodman's labels—names and predicates—for unacceptable entities. They are both, using the latter's terminology, *empty*. We might say that an illegitimate Native question imagines possible things that might be known (i.e., nonactual, impractical things), whereas an unacceptable entity by Goodman's lights (e.g., powers, dispositions, nonactual possibilia and the like) are imperceptible, hence their labels label nothing. In each case, the legitimacy or acceptability of a question or a label requires experiential content. In short: The American Indian world version is not empty; there are no Platonic forms—or their ilk—for either Goodman or Blue Jacket.

There is a perhaps more important Native justification for the limits of questioning principle. By most Western accounts, there are mathematical facts of the matter about the prime numbers, facts that are independent of knowers in the sense that Sally's motives for posing the question "Is there a greatest prime number?" are utterly irrelevant to the fact itself. Given the nature of the mathematical world—whether understood realistically or formalistically—mathematical facts are mind-independent entities to be *discovered*. Why a subject wants to discover them will not affect the outcome—what mathematician would believe otherwise? However, as noted earlier, the American Indian tradition constructs a world that is creative, animate, dynamic, purposeful, unfixed, and unfinished—a world in whose creation human beings participate. In such a moral universe where we are all related, the act of questioning and the motives behind the act shape a world in which *creativity* is the moving force. Real questions arise in a direct and practical action and performance, and actions and performances help to create a world that is still unfolding. Thus, one must be cautious and responsible—self-limiting, if you will—in the sorts of and motives for the questions one poses. Burkhart (2004) expresses this creative participation in making the world as the *meaning-shaping principle of action*, the last of his four epistemic principles (16–17).

Native Knowledge and Truth

In our earlier brief review of the JTB analysis of knowledge we noted that the Western conception of knowledge is principally propositional, and so the truth clause requires that the statement known be true. That is, however truth is analyzed it is a property of *statements*. We also have seen that American Indians consider procedural knowledge—knowing how to *p*—to be the principal kind of knowledge, and that procedural knowledge is somehow measured by the utility of an action, performance, or procedure in addressing some practical concern. This suggests, I maintain, that truth in the Native world version is a *property of action or performance*—not of statements—and that the truth of an action or performance must be understood in terms of its success in undertaking some endeavor, satisfying some desire or achieving some goal.

But we must remember, as Kristine Kurian reminds us, that merely satisfying a goal does not alone make an activity, procedure, or performance true. For, she observes:

> [I]f you compare the process of the Indian method planting the three sisters together in mounds you get corn. . . . And you could

plant in the same mounds for decades and beyond without loss of vigor to the plants or the soil. If you plant western method monoculture and irrigate and use synthetic fertilizers, you get tons of corn, but to the detriment of the aquatic life, and all down the food chain, etc. Ultimately the great harvest of western corn creates less food for the rest of those (not just people) on the planet. (1)

That is, if the goal is narrowly construed to be producing as much corn as possible, then Western industrial agriculture is the hands down winner in achieving the goal—at the expense, however, of the land and the rest of our relatives in the natural world. Indeed, only the hardest heart could imagine that achieving a goal—even if it harms or kills one's human relatives, let alone our nonhuman relatives—could be true. Otherwise, Captain Simeon Ecuyer's distribution of smallpox-infected blankets to a peaceful delegation of Lenni Lenape at Ft. Pitt during Pontiac's rebellion in 1763 was true, for it was wildly successful in achieving its goal—decimating the Delaware Nation (Eckert 2002: 490–91). So, in our analysis of a Native conception of truth we must make clear that the success in achieving any lesser goal must be informed by the principal overarching Indian goal—walking the right road—where all of our actions and performances in achieving the goal are mindful of our proper place in a web of normative relations with human and nonhuman persons. We might refer to this in shorthand as a *respectful* success in achieving a goal. Let us adopt, then, the following analysis:

For subject(s), S, her, his or their purpose or goal g, and action or performance p, p is true for S for g if and only if p is *respectfully successful* in achieving g.

As before, such actions and performances can be storytellings, healings, ceremonies, or simply observing the world to see connections between entities or events.[5]

Here are a few of the obvious consequences of the American Indian procedural conception of truth. First, because the respectful success in achieving a goal or purpose is a matter of degree, it follows that the truth of an action or performance is a matter of degree—a surprising result only if one is captivated by the Western tradition's bivalent notion of truth. But we've already seen that in the nondiscrete, complementary dualist logics embodied by indigenous thought the dualisms that may emerge—even the true and the false—are not regarded as opposites. Second, truth understood as a property of respectfully successful action—and not as correspondence to fact—sheds additional light on Burkhart's moral universe principle. "There is no difference between what is true and what is right," in a moral universe because all actions or performances have a moral content, and so actions or performances successful in walking the right road are also the ones that are right. Finally, the "subject" whose goal is successfully achieved can be an individual, group or even all of the People; indeed, not only Native truth but also knowledge is to be so understood, that is, an individual or the entire community is capable of knowing.

A story told by Dakota Ohiyesa, Dr. Charles Eastman (Fitzgerald 2007), in *The Soul of the Indian* illustrates the contrasting Western and Native conceptions of truth:

> A missionary once undertook to instruct a group of Indians in the truths of his holy religion. He told them of the creation of the earth in six days, and of the fall of our first parents by eating an apple.
>
> The courteous savages listened attentively, and after thanking him, one related in his turn a very ancient tradition concerning the origin of maize. But the missionary plainly showed his disgust and disbelief, indignantly saying: "What I delivered to you were sacred truths, but this that you tell me is mere fable and falsehood!"
>
> "My brother," gravely replied the offended Indian, "it seems that you have not been well grounded in the rules of civility. You saw that we, who practice these rules, believed your stories; why, then, do you refuse to credit ours?" (30)

Notice that the missionary declares his stories to be "sacred truths" but the Indian story to be "fable and falsehood." The reason is that according to his Western conceptions of truth and history there is a way the world is—a world of historical sacred facts—and a story is true only if it corresponds to these facts. If so, then there will be only one true origin story—the privileged one that gets the historical facts right—and all others, including the Native story, are false. On the other hand, according to the Native conception of truth an action or performance is true for an individual or group only if the action or performance respectfully and successfully achieves a goal. In this case, the performance is a speech act—the telling of an origin story—and the subject is the Native storyteller. In determining the goal of the subject we must ask, "What is the purpose in telling an origin story?" It is, by the way, manifestly *not* to express a historical sacred fact of the matter about the origin of the world that excludes and falsifies all other accounts.

As Fixico reminds us, there are many reasons for the telling of a story, the basis of Native oral traditions. A telling can put the experiences of the

People into perspective, helping to make sense of the situation in which they find themselves. The performance is the vehicle for traditional knowledge and moral values, and it sometimes sees the future. In conveying knowledge and values across generations, telling a story strengthens tribal bonds and ties to other creatures in the world. "Powerful and vivid," writes Fixico (2003), "each account is an entity of power" (22). In short, the telling of an origin story *centers* the People—it reminds them that "This is who you are and this is where you belong." In this particular performance recounted by Ohiyesa, the purpose of the Native storyteller was surely to try—out of respect—to convey all of this to the missionary; after all, the missionary had gifted his origin story to them.

Now, given that these two peoples have had different histories, values, traditions, and experiences, it naturally follows that the two storytellings—the two performances—will be different, yet equally true, if they each respectfully and successfully achieve the goal of putting the experiences of each group into perspective. We might imagine the offended Indian explaining to the missionary, "You saw that we believed your stories, because you need to tell a different sort of story to remind your people who they are and where they belong. Our knowledge, values, and experiences are different from yours, so our stories must be different. Why, then, do you refuse to credit ours?"

In support of the proposal that rehearsing an origin story is supposed to put the People's experiences into perspective, to make sense of circumstances befalling them, I offer the following. If there are radical reversals in the fortunes of the People—war, disease, deception, tribal division, and ultimately, removal—one would expect to hear corresponding changes in the performance of their origin story. This is exactly what we see in the Shawnee Prophet's narration of the Shawnee story in 1824.

Like other Eastern and Great Lakes tribes, by the early nineteenth century the Shawnee had endured disease, white encroachment, wars with Great Britain and the new American nation, tribal division, and removal to reservation lands. By the 1820s, the Shawnee lands in Ohio had been reduced to three small reservations occupied by one contingent of the Nation—led by Black Hoof—that had made peace with the Americans after the Treaty of Fallen Timbers in 1795. Other Shawnee who refused to treat moved to the Indiana Territory and eventually sided with the British during the war of 1812, settling around Fort Malden in Ontario after England's defeat. However, the Nation had already been grievously divided years earlier. The first great division of the Shawnee took place following the 1774 defeat in Dunmore's War. By 1780, when Tecumthe's home village, Piqua Town, was attacked by a large force of army regulars and Kentucky militia commanded by George Rogers Clark, a large contingent of Shawnee had already moved west to settle in eastern Missouri. And by the 1820s, many Shawnee leading men had been killed, including the murders of Cornstalk in 1777 under a flag of truce and Moluntha in 1786 while holding a signed treaty and displaying an American flag, and Tecumthe's fall in battle against William Henry Harrison on the Thames River in 1813 (Dabe 1994). If the purpose of an origin story is to put the experiences of the People into perspective, to help them to make sense of the situation in which they find themselves, then we should expect the early nineteenth-century Shawnee story to reflect this history of reversal.

In 1824, C. C. Trowbridge visited the Shawnee Prophet Tenskwa-tawa—Tecumthe's brother—probably at Detroit but possibly at his home at Fort Malden. Tenskwatawa—meaning "Open Door"—shared with Trow-bridge the Shawnee origin story; and, after telling how the first Shawnee were made in the sky by the Great Spirit, Weisamanitoo—with a piece of His own heart—the Prophet told the following:

> The Great spirit then opened a door, and looking down they saw a white man seated upon the ground. He was naked, and destitute of hair upon his head or his body and had been cir-cumcised. The great Spirit told them that this white man was not made by himself but by another spirit who made & governed the whites & over whom or whose subjects he had no controul. That as soon as they reached their Island and had got comfortably situated, this great white spirit would endeavour to thwart his designs, and would certainly exert himself to change the period of their existence from 200 years to a shorter time. (Trowbridge in Kinietz and Voegelin 1939: 3; all textual idiosyncrasies are faithful to the original)

What we see, I believe, is an addition to the Shawnee origin narrative intended to make sense of the evils that had befallen the Nation at the hands of whites, for it is pretty unlikely that this was a part of the story before contact with Europeans. Whites had been created and governed by another great white spirit whose purpose was to interfere with Weisamanitoo and the Shawnee people. We might also infer that it reflects a measure of disdain for Christianity—the religion of the great white spirit; unsurprising, for Tenskwatawa's message to the Shawnee—like that of many Indian "mes-siahs"—was to eschew white ways and return to Native traditions.

Clearly, we cannot ignore some of the Shawnee Prophet's other pos-sible goals, including making the fool of Trowbridge by concocting a story. I doubt this, however, since Trowbridge also interviewed Chief Black Hoof at the Ohio reservation Wapaghkonetta, and Black Hoof's narration of the

Shawnee origin story corresponds to Tenskwatawa's in several important respects. Interestingly enough, Black Hoof's telling does not include a second great white spirit intending to thwart the designs of Weisamanitoo, but it still makes clear that Christianity—a religion made for the whites—was not made for the Shawnee:

> [The whites] endeavored to convince [the Shawnee] of the propriety of embracing the christian religion, but the red men replied that the Great spirit had already furnished them with a religion suited to their nature and capacity, that they were perfectly satisfied with it, that they might reciprocate the offer of their religion to the whites with propriety, but they thought it best for each to keep the ways which the Great spirit had given them.[6] (Trowbridge: 63; all textual idiosyncrasies are faithful to the original)

Although different from Tenskwatawa's narration in how it tries to account for the Shawnee reversals at the hands of whites, Black Hoof's telling still reminds the People who they are and where they belong, just as a *true* performance of an origin story should.

The *Black Elk* narrative provides to us one last observation about the Native conception of truth. After Black Elk (2000) tells the story about how White Buffalo Woman brought the sacred pipe to the Lakota, he reflects that, "This they tell, and whether it happened so or not I do not know; but if you think about it, you can see that it is true" (4). Now, the Western epistemologist who believes that truth is correspondence to fact puzzles at this apparent contradiction; Black Elk doesn't know if "it happened or not"—whether the story corresponds to an actual event—but "if you think about it, you can see that it is true"—*that the story corresponds to an actual event!* Moreover, the epistemologist wonders how merely reflecting on the story could verify such a correspondence. However, Black Elk is *not* incoherent, for it is perfectly consistent to admit that he doesn't know whether the story is factual, but to recognize that telling the story can successfully achieve the goal of conveying the sanctity and symbolism of the pipe and the pipe ceremony in a respectful manner.

Native Knowledge and Verification

We have been considering an American Indian conception of knowledge because of Deloria's opening observation that the Native approach to understanding the world differs from a Western methodology in its ultimate goal—to find the right road for a human being to walk—and in the kinds of experiences that count as evidence. Having just completed a discussion of an American Indian conception of truth, an important component of knowledge and a first requirement of a culturally sophisticated interpretation of inductive rightness, we now turn to a discussion of verification—again, because verification is an important component of knowledge, and because a second requirement of inductive rightness is having all genuine evidence available.

Intuitively, verification within a procedural conception of knowledge should involve one verifying the success in achieving a goal or purpose by acting or performing in some way, that is, one directly experiencing the *utility* of an action or performance. As in our consideration of a procedural conception of truth, the action or performance can be as elaborate as a ceremony or as simple as searching for connections between entities or events. But we must be very cautious here, for this notion of "direct experience" is not consonant with the Western empirical method of verification, which tries to exclude anomalous or unique, private or nonempirical experiences. Only experiences that are objective and can be replicated count as evidence, because the Western method is *exclusionary* (Deloria 1999: 44). This is not surprising, for the underlying assumption about the natural world held by most in the Western tradition is that it is an inert, mechanistic, and material place, whose causal operations are governed by mathematically formulated physical laws. So an anomalous, nonobjective experience—a unique experience that cannot be shared with others—must not be *genuine* evidence because it is private and not law-like. However, the American Indian method of verification is *inclusive*, for no experience—even the uniquely personal or mysteriously anomalous—is discarded in formulating their understanding of the world. "Everything had to be included in the spectrum of knowledge and related to what was already known" (Deloria 1999: 44). Thus arises the belief—long misunderstood and derided by the Western tradition—that visions, dreams, intuitions, and other sorts of experiences that transcend the merely objective and replicable can count as *genuine evidence*.[7]

A Western mind wonders how such unusual experiences—visions, dreams, and intuitions among them—could possibly count as genuine evidence. Indeed, I've found that the almost universal Western response to Black Elk's powerful life-changing vision, induced by an illness when he was nine, ranges from extreme skepticism to derision (Black Elk 2000: 16–36). No less incredible is the story Black Elk tells about Drinks Water's prophetic dream:

A long time ago my father told me what his father told him,
that there was once a Lakota holy man, called Drinks Water,

who dreamed what was to be; and this was long before the
coming of the [whites]. He dreamed that the four-leggeds were
going back into the earth and that a strange race had woven a
spider's web all around the Lakotas. And he said: "When this
happens, you shall live in square gray houses, in a barren land,
and beside those square houses you shall starve." They say he
went back to Mother Earth soon after he saw this vision, and
it was sorrow that killed him. You can look about you now
and see that he meant these dirt-roofed houses we are living
in, and that all the rest was true. Sometimes dreams are wiser
than waking. (8)

By Native lights, Drinks Water had a profoundly insightful experience that cannot be dismissed, one that must be included in the spectrum
of knowledge, because dreams can be "wiser than waking." But how can
a dream count as evidence for anything—except, perhaps, that American
Indians have a primitive and undeveloped conception of verification?
To understand the Native conception of verification we must consider
the deceptively pregnant notion of the direct experience of the success of
an action or performance. Recall that one of our principal constructivist
premises is that there is no such thing as a bare fact, because all facts
are *fabricated*. Likewise, there is no such thing as a direct experience of a
bare fact, because all experiences are *interpreted*, that is, mediated by some
model, theory, or world version. As we now know quite well, facts—and our
experiences of them—are constructed and verified within a cultural frame of
reference, be it the Western scientific frame or the American Indian world
version. Comparing these two different culturally governed ways of framing
the world, Fixico (2003) observes that "the Indian mind is more accepting
of the truth and facts, [while] the Western linear mind must pursue empirical evidence to prove something is true so that it can become factual in
the scientific sense" (9).
How, then, do we understand Native direct experience, and what is
the nature of the American Indian world version that informs it? And why
should the Indian mind be more "accepting of the truth and facts" than the
Western mind? I believe there are two components to the Native perspective that inform direct experience: (1) the absence of a skepticism about
the veracity of any and all experience, and (2) the first common theme that
relatedness is a world-ordering principle.
One of the oldest distinctions in the Western tradition is that between
appearance and reality. We see it in Thales' sixth-century B.C.E. ontological proposal that everything in reality is water, for material objects like the
table before me certainly do not appear to be water. Moreover, the distinc-

tion is still with us, for the table before me doesn't appear to be a mass of imperceptibly small particles in motion, but that's what modern science tells us it *really* is. Thus, it has been widely held in the Western tradition that our experiences of the world—the ways the world appears to us—are often deceptive; no wonder it has been long concerned with devising tests—both philosophical and scientific—to determine just when an experience is veritable, when it corresponds to and conveys information about the *real* world. But whatever test one adopts, it is a truism in the Western epistemological tradition that dreams, visions, and the like are deceptive experiences; they correspond to nothing in the *real* world. While experiences are, in general, suspect, these kinds of experiences are *never* veritable.

On the other hand, the Western tradition's sharp distinction between appearance and reality—as well as its conviction that some kinds of experiences are inherently unreliable or deceiving—are largely absent from the American Indian tradition. For Native people, the experience one has at any particular moment, including the prophetic dream or the mysterious religious experience, when interpreted in light of a long-evolving world version, *is* reality. There is no hidden real world distinctly different from the world that appears to us; to believe so—as Western thinkers do—Deloria (1999) calls a "superstition":

> Indians never had a need to posit the existence of a "real" reality beyond the senses because they felt that their senses gave them the essence of physical existence. . . . What could be more superstitious than to believe that the world in which we live and where we have our most intimate personal experiences is not really trustworthy and that another, mathematical world exists that represents a true reality? (39)

As well, there are no inherently unreliable or deceptive experiences' in the American Indian world version. Black Elk's powerful vision and Drinks Water's prophetic dream are not immediately rejected because they are anomalous, mysterious, or private, but are instead interpreted in terms of and integrated into an ever-evolving body of knowledge held in common by the People. Importantly, such experiences are not regarded as different in kind from waking experiences, but as providing evidence for other "dimensions to life" besides the waking life:

> If there were other dimensions to life—the religious experiences and dreams certainly indicated the presence of other ways of living, even other places—they were regarded as part of an organic whole and not as distinct from other experiences, times,

and places in the same way that Western thinkers have always believed. (Deloria 1999: 39)

Hallowell (1960) concurs in his study of the Ojibwa, a "dream-conscious people." Unlike Westerners, who include only waking experiences when thinking autobiographically, the Ojibwa integrate both waking and dream experiences into their self-narrative; indeed, dream experiences are often considered to be far more important than waking experiences.

The first component, then, of the Native perspective that informs direct experience is the absence of a skepticism about the veracity of any and all experience, including dream and religious experiences. As important, however, is the belief that all entities, events, and activities—including those experienced in one's nonwaking life—are related; *we would say that relationships between various sorts of experiences are created*. According to Fixico (2003), the perspective of a cultural system that regards everything as related sees beyond the human sphere, "involv[ing] human beings, animals, plants, the natural environment, and *the metaphysical world of visions and dreams*" (2, emphasis added). Of course, direct experience, so informed, constructs relationships between tangible physical beings; but it also perceives relationships between the physical and the realm Fixico terms the "metaphysical": " 'Seeing' involves mentally experiencing the relationships between tangible and nontangible things in the world and in the universe. . . . It is acceptance of fact that a relationship exists between a tangible item like a mountain and a dream" (3).

Given the veracity of all forms of experience and the relationships between waking and dream experiences, it is no wonder that Drinks Water died from despair upon recognizing a relationship between his dream experiences and the future of his People. And given the absence of skepticism about the veracity of a wide variety of experiences, it is no wonder that the American Indian mind is more "accepting of the truth and facts" than the Western mind, which, we've noted, has a skeptical attitude about experience.

We began with the notion that verification within a procedural conception of knowledge should involve someone directly experiencing the utility of an action or performance, and in our examination of direct experience in the American Indian world version we found that Native people have a high confidence in the veracity of experiences of all sorts. What happens, then, if individuals have very different experiences with respect to the utility of an action, performance, or procedure?

We cannot say, as Burkhart (2004) points out, that one individual's experiences are more privileged than another's, for "[w]hat place do I have to tell you that your experiences are invalid because I do not share them?" (26). Instead, each individual's experiences—as well as those embodied by tribal tradition—must be taken into account. "A Native philosophical understanding," he shares, "must include all experience, not simply my own. If I am to gain a right understanding I must account for all that I see, but also all that you see and all that has been seen by others—all that has been passed down in stories" (25–26). You see, in an American Indian world that is animate and interconnected, dynamic and purposeful, unfixed and unfinished, it is not inconsistent for experiences to vary from person to person. And because no individual's experiences are privileged, because any experience can count as evidence, a right understanding of the dynamic world requires a synthesis of diverse experiences in light of the evolving body of tribal knowledge. As Burkhart observes, the messiness of the data, replete with apparent contradictions and anomalies, can make understanding difficult. However, in a world we help to create, understanding is an ongoing process; to stop thinking and observing, to cease the search for connections between experiences—even between tangible and intangible entities, events, and actions—is to end the process prematurely (Burkhart 2004: 25).

It appears as though the focus of our consideration of Native verification has been exclusively on the individual, somewhat like its Western counterpart, the justification clause of the JTB analysis of knowledge. Indeed, we noticed earlier that the Western epistemological analysis of knowledge itself assumes that the definition of knowledge is formulated in terms of conditions met by individual knowers. However, we have throughout made an implicit reference to *tribal knowledge*, the practical knowledge accumulated and held by the community over generations, and disseminated to the young by tribal elders through teaching and story, advice and counsel. Thus, our consideration of an American Indian conception of verification cannot ignore tribal tradition—the authority of communal knowledge—in verifying the utility of an action, performance, or procedure.[8]

Given our reflections about verification in the Native world version, I propose the following analysis:

> For subject(s), S, her, his or their purpose or goal g, and action or performance p, p is justified or verified for S for g if and only if either (1) S directly experiences the respectful success of p in achieving g, or (2) the respectful success of p in achieving g is endorsed by S's tribal tradition.

Black Elk's narrative provides examples of each alternative. First, for a subject and goal, an action or performance is verified if the subject directly experiences the utility of the action or performance. Black Elk (2000) tells of his first cure, when, after having been led to a medicinal herb he saw in a vision, used the herb in a ceremony to heal a sick child. That is, Black Elk, the subject, directly experienced the success of his first healing ceremony in achieving the goal of curing the boy (150–56). Second, the narrative shows us the heyoka ceremony, whose goal is to return the People to spiritual equilibrium, to lift their spirits when they are in despair and to sober them "when they feel too good and are too sure of being safe," and whose utility was endorsed by tribal tradition (Black Elk 2000: 145–49).

As a final reflection, I think nothing highlights the difference between American Indian and Western conceptions of verification more than the observation that the two ways of verifying the utility of an action or procedure in the Native world version—an individual's direct experience and the endorsement of tradition—are regarded as fallacious sources of evidence by Western lights. Appealing to someone's direct experience as evidence commits the aesthetic fallacy, for the West is skeptical about the veracity of private experience. Moreover, looking to tradition for verification commits the appeal to authority fallacy, for the mere fact that a belief is entrenched or well established is alone insufficient evidence for its truth. American Indians have a confidence in the veracity of experiences of all sorts, a regard for tribal knowledge and a respect for the wisdom of elders that the Western worldview lacks.[9]

Native Knowledge and Ultimate Acceptability

We have been examining Native notions of truth and verification in order to understand the American Indian procedural conception of knowledge, which, I suggest, may be analyzed as follows. Keeping in mind that knowers can be individuals or groups, that actions or performances can be elaborate ceremonies or simple observations, and that the most important goal is finding the right road for a human being to walk, which requires true performances to be respectfully successful:

> For subject(s), S, her, his or their purpose or goal g, and action or performance, p, S knows how to p to achieve g if and only if (1) p is true for S for g, and (2) p is justified or verified for S for g.

Our investigation of truth and verification also contributes to the argument that an American Indian world version constructs an actual world. For true versions construct well-made actual worlds, and ultimate acceptability is sufficient for truth. And, given a culturally sophisticated interpretation of Goodman's criteria for the ultimate acceptability of a world version, an American Indian world version is ultimately acceptable.

The criteria for ultimate acceptability include deductive and inductive rightness, utility and nonemptiness, and our recent reflections indicate that all standards of rightness except nonemptiness must be interpreted within a cultural frame of reference. First of all, Anne Waters (2004a) investigated the logical system within which Native deductive inferences take place; she has illuminated for us the standard of deductive rightness·

We, however, have spent a good deal of time considering aspects of the American Indian cultural frame of reference important to interpreting inductive rightness. We grant, with Goodman, that right induction requires true premises and the availability of all genuine evidence; all confirming instances must be available and no negative instances can be omitted. Right projection then depends on the right categorization of experience, organizing experience into relevant kinds entrenched by habit. Employing *relatedness as a world-ordering principle*, Natives construct a moral universe that is interconnected and dynamic, a world in whose creation human beings participate through their thoughts, actions, and ceremonies. In such a world, categorization cannot be static and projection must be cautious, necessitating an ongoing process of verification. Like Western right induction, all genuine evidence must be available, but Natives do not arbitrarily exclude some experiences because they are inherently deceptive; all experiences, even the anomalous, mysterious, or private can count as genuine evidence.

We saw that the American Indian conception of truth is principally procedural—not propositional—and is tied to practical concerns that are close at hand. So, the utility of an action, performance, or procedure is a crucial condition for truth, and, in turn, the utility of the Native world version must be a criterion for its ultimate acceptability. And the American Indian version *was* useful; it helped human beings achieved the goal of walking the right road. Indeed, it is interesting to note that the principal message of most Native messiah movements—like the Shawnee Prophet's and Wovoka's—is that Indians need to eschew the Western ways and beliefs that brought them ill-fortune and return to their Native ways as practiced before contact with European colonial powers, because they flourished under the old ways.

Finally, because the American Indian world version is pragmatic and based in direct experiences of all sorts, it is not an empty version. In fact, we suggested that Brian Burkhart's limits of questioning principle helps secure the Native world version *against* emptiness. I conclude, then, that because the American Indian version satisfies culturally interpreted standards of deductive and inductive rightness, utility and nonemptiness, it is an ultimately acceptable version. And, given that ultimate acceptability is a sufficient condition for truth, and true versions construct well-made actual worlds, the American Indian world is an actual, well-made world. So, rather than being "a mass of nonsense, a mass of incoherent folly," as ethnographer Powell judges (1877: 13), the Native world version is worthy of philosophical treatment—and respect—from the Western perspective.

5

An Expansive Conception
of Persons

This chapter begins with the insightful critique of a prominent Western conception of persons by Ross Poole, which will nicely frame our development of an American Indian expansive conception of persons. We will find that human beings are essentially "spirit beings" in a changeable human form who become persons by virtue of their relationships with and obligations to other persons in a social group that is more closely related to a family than to a Western civil society. Unlike Western conceptions, however, we will see that the Native conception of persons is *expansive*, for all sorts of nonhuman spirit beings—ancestors and animals, plants and places, physical forces and cardinal directions, the Sun, Earth, and other powerful spirit beings—are members of the American Indian familial community, and so are persons.

A Western Conception of Persons

In Chapter 1 we noted the deeply ingrained Western conviction—reinforced by science, religion, and common sense—that human beings are different in kind from other nonhuman animals, but that cultural anthropologists and ethnographers often observe that American Indian traditions regard human beings and other nonhuman animals as in some way equal. "They do not separate man from the beast," says J. W. Powell (1877), "[s]o the Indian speaks of 'our race' as of the same rank with the bear race, the wolf race or the rattlesnake race" (10). But we will see that what Powell regards as a "very curious and interesting fact" is an often-repeated misinterpretation undoubtedly born of an imposition of Western categories and prejudices on the American Indian worldview. Instead, I will argue that a recurring theme in Native traditions is an expansive conception of persons, in which nonhuman animals—and other sorts of other-than-human beings—are recognized as persons in a sense as or more robust than a Western conception of human persons. Thus, the value of human beings is not diminished, but the value of other kinds of entities in the world is enhanced. It is not that "[m]ankind is supposed simply to be one of the many races of animals" in Native worldviews—as Powell haughtily asserts—but that Indians regard the many races of animals to be people like humankind:

> Behind the apparent kinship between animals, reptiles, birds, and human beings in the Indian way stands a great conception shared by a great majority of the tribes. Other living things are not regarded as insensitive species. Rather they are "people" in the same manner as the various tribes of human beings are people. The reason why the Hopi use live retiles in their ceremony goes back to one of their folk heroes who lived with the snake people for a while and learned from them the secret of making rain for the crops. . . . In the same manner the Plains Indians considered the buffalo as a distinct people, the Northwest Coast Indians regarded the salmon as a people. (Deloria 1994: 89–90)

A Native expansive conception of persons in which not only animals but plants and places, physical forces and cardinal directions, even the Sun, Moon, and Earth are persons is clearly different from various Western conceptions in which being human is a necessary condition for personhood. Indeed, the commonsense notion of a person, as captured by everyday usage, is telling: A person is "a human being, whether man, woman, or child . . . as distinguished from an animal or a thing" ("person" 2004). And according to Irving Hallowell (1960), persons and human beings are categorically identified in psychology and the social sciences (21).

Thankfully, philosophers have been a little more careful and reflective in their attribution of personhood to or identification of persons with human beings. In fact, a widely embraced contemporary philosophical view—with roots in John Locke and Immanuel Kant—has it that being human is *not* essential to being a person. After rehearsing the historical and conceptual development of this view, Ross Poole (1996) poses an interesting Hegelian sort of challenge that will shed light both on the Western and American Indian conceptions of a person.

Poole argues that John Locke's notion of a person entrenched an earlier Hobbesian conception, which was informed in turn by an even older Roman notion that to be a person is to take on a public role—to be a full subject of the law and thereby have legal rights and duties, as well as to have the right to participate in certain public rituals and ceremonies (39).

Hobbes' transitional view incorporates this older notion that a person is one who has the legal right to act on the public stage with the dawning idea that a person is also "the inner being of the agent who occupied the role," as Poole puts it. Thus, Hobbes melds the earlier tradition that rights and obligations are grounded in one's person qua public entity with the idea that "person" refers to some intrinsic nature of the one playing that public role (40). It seems, then, that Hobbes began to combine the two components of personhood that Daniel Dennett (1978) finds in John Locke's later account, namely, a *moral* notion and a *metaphysical* notion.

In developing the metaphysical component of personhood, Locke (1991) famously distinguishes the idea of a person from the idea of a man (i.e., a human animal). The identity of a man over time is understood as "the same Animal . . . the same continued Life communicated to different Particles of Matter, as they happen successively to be united to that organiz'd living Body" (332–33). On the other hand, Locke proposes that *any* self-reflective rational being can be a person, and that the identity of a person over time is a function of a being's conscious identification of recollected past selves with its present self:

> [T]o find wherein *personal Identity* consists, we must consider what *Person* stands for; which, I think, is a thinking intelligent Being, that has reason and reflection, and can consider it self as it self, the same thinking thing in different times and places; which it does only by that consciousness, which is inseparable for thinking, and as it seems to me essential to it. (335)

However, Locke also is concerned about the legal and moral responsibilities and rewards incurred by and due to persons—just as Hobbes was—and he locates these in a second moral component of personhood, where, as Dennett observes, the metaphysical notion of a person as a special kind of self-reflective rational being appears to be a necessary condition for that being's moral accountability. For, one can take credit or blame for some past action only if one appropriates the past action as one's own—and that requires consciously identifying a past self with the present self:

> ["Person"] is a Forensick Term appropriating Actions and their Merit; and so belongs only to intelligent Agents capable of a Law, and Happiness and Misery. This personality extends it *self* beyond present Existence to what is past, only by consciousness, whereby it becomes concerned and accountable, owns and imputes to it *self* past Actions, just upon the same ground, and for the same reason, that it does the present. (Locke 1991: 346)

Poole (1996) nicely summarizes the Lockean person as the self-conscious, language using, corporeal, rational being who is "cognizant of and thus subject to the demands of law and morality"—an amalgam of the metaphysical and moral notions—*but not the human organism at all*. As such, in Locke's view not all human beings are persons; and, Poole importantly observes, "it is at least conceptually possible that some nonhuman animals might be counted as persons" (40–41).

The distinction between persons and human beings is more sharply drawn by Kant, who developed the concept of a person as a moral agent wholly independent of actual facts about human beings. Moral laws are universal and necessary, so they cannot be mere empirical generalizations we might make about actual human behavior, since an empirical generalization can be falsified by a single disconfirming instance. However, moral laws are never falsified by actual human actions and circumstances; despite the fact that human beings actually murder, the moral imperative "Thou shalt not murder" is still true and necessarily binding on all moral agents—that is, binding on all *persons*. Now, the only way Kant (1964) can account for such universal, apodictic imperatives—and a person's categorical duty to obey them—is by ignoring altogether the contingencies arising from particular human desires and inclinations, and grounding the moral law in *reason*. As such, the moral law is necessarily binding not just on human beings, but also on any rational creature whatsoever:

> Every one must admit that a law has to carry with it absolute
> necessity if it is to be valid morally—valid, that is, as a ground
> of obligation; that the command "Thou shalt not lie" could not
> hold merely for men, other rational beings having no obligation
> to abide by it—and similarly with all other genuine moral laws;
> that here consequently the ground of obligation must be looked
> for, not in the nature of man nor in the circumstances of the
> world in which he is placed, but solely *a priori* in the concepts
> of pure reason. (57)

So, as Poole observes, it is not the contingencies of our actual human nature or situation that makes us persons in Kant's view. Reason makes us persons; and by virtue of our reason—imperfect though it may be—we are creatures with an intrinsic value. So, Kant identifies our rational nature as what we are essentially, and he abstracts that which is essential to us—our personhood—from our humanity (44–45).

After tracing the development of the view that being human is not essential to personhood through contemporary philosophers Frankfurt (1971), Dennett (1976), and Nerlich (1989), Poole (1996) argues that something has gone awry: Philosophers in the Lockean/Kantian tradition begin by identifying certain features they take to be essential to personhood—perhaps moral agency, self-consciousness, or rationality—and then observe that not every human being has that essential feature, so being human is not sufficient for being a person. Nor is it necessary, for one can imagine other sorts of nonhuman beings with these essential features. Therefore, they conclude, being human is neither necessary nor sufficient for personhood; being a person is thus wholly abstracted from a particular kind of existence—*a human existence* (46–47).

Poole proposes instead that the interesting sorts of features various philosophers have identified that distinguish persons from other kinds of things—moral agency, rationality, language use, and self-awareness among them—arose from, hence *cannot be understood apart from*, a specific kind of organic, social life that gave rise to them in the first place. Self-consciousness—Locke's criterion of personhood—is an embodied *human* self-consciousness; rationality—Kant's criterion—is an embodied *human* rationality; moral agency—their common concern—is a *human* moral agency constituted by a human being's actual participation in a network of human social and political practices and relationships. Indeed, one's *personal* identity is a special kind of *social* identity. Ignoring this, Poole (1996) argues, leads to the "calamitous consequence" in moral philosophy that persons, as the bearers of moral rights and responsibilities, are abstracted from the very concrete, human situations that engender moral dilemmas in the first place—including abortion, capital punishment, euthanasia, and consuming nonhuman animals (48–51). Our attention is instead drawn toward concerns about our moral obligations to Vulcans, machines passing the Turing test or any similar nonhuman "persons" in the fantasy world of thought experiments.

Importantly, Poole (1996) argues against the metaphysical notion that personhood—however conceived—is our *essential* being, because there are all sorts of interesting features about human beings besides the usual candidates for personhood that could reasonably serve as the core of a conception of persons, so no one of them should be identified as that which is essential to being human:

> Cognitive scientists, for example, may be more impressed with our capacity to draw and evaluate certain kinds of inference, than the fact that we can dance or make love, so they construct a concept of a person on the basis of these preferred attributes. In itself this move is harmless enough, and may even be useful in certain contexts. But we should be wary of assuming that this concept signifies what we most essentially are. (55–56)

Likewise, we should be wary of the seemingly plausible proposals that our essential being is constituted by personhood construed as self-awareness, rationality, or moral agency—even participating in a certain kind of social and moral life. Because there are so many attributes that could serve as the core of personhood, identifying any one attribute as our *essential being* is unjustified.

Perhaps remarkably, we will find elements of Poole's Western development of the concept of a person in our consideration of an American Indian expansive conception of personhood. First, human beings are not persons by nature; that which makes them persons cannot be abstracted from a particular, concrete kind of existence. Human beings become persons—and sustain their identity as persons—by virtue of their participation in certain forms of social practices and performances, and through their relationships with and obligations to other persons. Second, the social practices and performances, relationships and obligations that engender and sustain human beings as persons are *moral* in nature, that is, moral agency is at the core of personhood. Finally, being a person is not what is essential to being human. However, we will see that these three elements are entirely consistent with the view that *there are nonhuman persons!*

Native Conceptions of Animate Beings and Persons

We begin with the now familiar traditional Native story of "Coyote, Iktome, and the Rock," told by Jenny Leading Cloud (Erdoes and Ortiz 1984). It has versions in at least the Lakota, Blackfoot, and Apache traditions, and it has even slipped into popular Western culture. It will serve as a touchstone as we clarify the American Indian notion of a human being as an animate being, the Native *expansive conception of persons*, and the important difference between them.

As the story goes, Coyote and Iktome were going about in their usual way when they came upon Iya—a quite old and powerful Rock—and Coyote (quite uncharacteristically) gifted him his thick woolen blanket. In response to Iktome's surprise, Coyote replied: "It's nothing. I'm always giving things away. Iya looks real nice in my blanket."

"*His* blanket, now," Iktome reminded.

Well, the weather turned off wet and cold, and the pair took refuge in a cave. Coyote, without his warm blanket, was freezing, so he sent Iktome back to retrieve the blanket from Iya. The Rock rebuffed him saying, "No, what is given is given!"

Coyote was beside himself when Iktome returned empty handed, so he confronted Iya himself—and he took back the gifted blanket.

"So there; that's the end of it," Coyote said.

"By no means the end," said the Rock.

Coyote returned to the cave with the blanket and found Iktome fixing a lunch of pemmican and fry-bread. The pair dined and then settled down for a smoke to enjoy the fair weather that followed the storm when they heard a rumble that shook the very ground. It was Iya, returning to retrieve his blanket.

"Friend, let's run for it!" cried Iktome. "Iya means to kill us!"

Iya chased Coyote and Iktome across the river and through the woods; Iya's power enabled him to swim the river as though he were made of wood, and to splinter trees left and right in the forest. Iktome recognized the peril and "excused" himself, turning into a spider and scampering down a mouse hole.

Iya caught Coyote—and rolled right over him, squashing him flat. After collecting his blanket, the Rock returned to his place, saying, "What is given is given." (Leading Cloud, in Erdoes and Ortiz 1984: 337–39).

Coyote is a Trickster in many Native traditions; his role is played by Raven and Hare in others. One of Trickster's many purposes in stories is to show most graphically what is bound to happen when one forgets one's proper place, failing to be mindful of one's relationships with and responsibilities to others, or giving into one's own desires at the expense of others. When Trickster acts on impulse, is greedy, vain, sometimes just mindlessly self-absorbed—or when he reclaims a gifted blanket—then he disrupts a delicate equilibrium between persons in a dynamic network of relationships sustained by mutual respect, courtesy, and equality. This should be his lesson—and we should learn as well, for we all too often act in the same ways (Martin 1999: 59–62). It often ends badly for Coyote; but like his contemporary animated relative, Wiley Coyote, he seems always to recover—and never to learn from his missteps. Iktome, the Spider person, is usually the butt of laughter—human, plant, and animal alike—because he always seeks shortcuts; Deloria (1999) shares that his stories teach humility and "the consequences of attempting to be what one is not supposed to be"[1] (26).

The first misconception to dispel is that these and like powerful nonhuman spirit persons are *gods* as understood in Western religious traditions.[2] For, if they were such entities, then they would be quite different from human beings in kind—they would be supernatural, infallible, and omnipotent. But there is, first of all, no distinction between the *natural* and the *supernatural* in the American Indian world version. According to Hallowell (1960), one does not find this fundamental Western distinction in the Native worldview because there is no analogue of the concept of the *natural world*—understood as an inanimate material world governed by fixed physical laws—in American Indian traditions. Using the example of the

Ojibwa conception of *gizis*, the "day luminary," Hallowell observes that the sun is not a *natural* object in the Western sense; it is a nonhuman person. So, he concludes, if the concept of the *natural* is absent, so must be the concept of the *supernatural*. Considering powerful nonhuman spirit persons to be "supernatural persons," he says,

> ... is completely misleading, if for no other reason than the fact that the concept of "supernatural" presupposes a concept of the "natural." The latter is not present in Ojibwa thought. It is unfortunate that the natural–supernatural dichotomy has been so persistently invoked by many anthropologists in describing the outlook of peoples in cultures other than our own. (28)

Deloria (1999) concurs in his reflections about how Western thinkers separate the material and the spiritual—that is, the natural and the supernatural—into two realms. "We are not dealing, therefore, with a conception of nature in the same way that Western thinkers conceive of things" (357). So, without a conception of the supernatural, it is obvious that powerful nonhuman spirit persons in American Indian traditions cannot be *supernatural gods*.

Nor are they infallible; indeed, if the story about Coyote, Iktome and Iya doesn't make clear that these powerful spirit persons can make mistakes, the Shawnee origin story does. As Tenskwatawa, the Shawnee Prophet, told it to Trowbridge:

> When the Great spirit made this Island he thought it necessary to make also human beings to inhabit it, and with this view he formed an Indian. After making him he caused him to stand erect, and having surveyed him from head to foot he pronounced the work defective, and made another, which he examined in the same manner with great care and particularity and at length pronounced him well made & perfect. (Kinietz and Voegelin 1; all idiosyncrasies are faithful to the text)

But this second creation was still defective, for the Great Spirit had placed the "privates" under the arm of the man and the woman. After some reflection—and vexation—he rearranged the different members of the body, "and at last made them as they now are, and was satisfied." Unlike infallible Western deities, the Great Spirit's first two human creations were mistakes; like humans, it took multiple tries—a little *practice*—to finally get it right.

So, Coyote, Iktome, Iya and other powerful nonhuman spirit persons
are neither supernatural nor infallible; and although quite powerful, they
are not *omnipotent*. Recall that Tenskwatawa informs Trowbridge that white
men were made by another spirit over whom he had no control. In short,
then, these Indian powerful nonhuman spirit entities are not supernatural
godlike deities; they are, we will see, no different *in kind* than human beings,
although they differ in power.

Now, this account began with the universal American Indian belief
that entities like Coyote, Iktome, and Iya are nonhuman spirit persons in
order to consider how they are like and unlike human beings and human persons—for the two are not equivalent. Doing so will help us begin to understand both human beings and personhood in American Indian traditions.
First, to similarities: Coyote, Iktome, and Iya all have, to a greater or lesser
extent, some of the attributes of human beings qua *animate* beings. Coyote
and Iktome eat pemmican and fry-bread, smoke pipes, and shiver in the
cold, just like we do. Moreover, they have needs and desires, as well as the
rationality and volition to satisfy them. More importantly, Coyote, Iktome,
and Iya participate in a network of social and moral practices and relationships, just as human *persons* do. Coyote and Iktome are friends—although
the Spider Person will not stand with his friend when "the chips are down";
Coyote has moral obligations to Iya—although he ignores those obligations
by taking back his gifted blanket. They speak and scheme together, and they
make mistakes in dealing with others—just as human persons do—and bear
the consequences of those missteps.

There are also obvious differences between these powerful nonhuman
spirit persons and human beings and human persons. The first and most
obvious difference is that, contrary to Poole's Western philosophical notion,
Coyote, Iktome, and Iya are *nonhuman* persons, although they can assume
human form. And it is far less obvious from outward appearances that Iya
has any of the attributes of a human being—let alone a person—until, of
course, the rock acts on the *moral* impulse to retrieve his blanket—the
kind of impulse on which a *person* would act. And it *is* a moral impulse;
Iya's motive is *righting a wrong*, not merely regaining the blanket he really
doesn't need, for "What is given is given." Second, Coyote, Iktome, and Iya
are extraordinarily powerful entities—indeed, apparently far more powerful
than human beings. Although a huge boulder, Iya is able to swim a river as
though he were made of wood and then smash a forest, "splintering the big
pines to pieces"; Iktome has the power to transform himself into a spider and
escape down a mouse hole; and Coyote—although smashed flat by Iya—has
the power to "make himself come to life again." Great power, then, seems
to be an attribute of these nonhuman spirit persons.

Because we adopted the American Indian belief that Coyote, Iktome, and Iya are nonhuman spirit persons at the outset, it should be clear that we will not agree with Poole that being human is a necessary condition for personhood in Native traditions. However, in our development of an American Indian expansive conception of persons we can embrace his other fundamental insights that (1) personhood does not constitute the essence of a human being; (2) an entity is a person by virtue of its membership and participation in a network of social and moral relationships and practices with other persons; and (3) moral agency is at the core of personhood. There are, then, two questions that need to be carefully distinguished as we proceed. First, what is essential to being human qua *animate entity* in the Native worldview? This is what human beings will share with nonhuman spirit persons, because they are animate beings too. Second, what do Indians believe is essential to *personhood*? Human persons will share this with Coyote, Iktome, and Iya, because they are persons—as well as animate beings.[3]

First, human beings qua animate beings are essentially *spirit beings*—who just happen to have a changeable outward human form—and it is this that human beings have in common with other animate beings. It usually is at this juncture that the skeptical Western scientific and philosophical minds guffaw, then disengage, because the claim has nothing but the air of the supernatural—which endangers, by the way, our constructivist claim that the American Indian world version is nonempty. For, apparently one cannot perceive a spirit, so the predicate "spirit" is as empty as other empty predicates—"angel," "devil," and "possible entity" among them—in Goodman's gallery of rogues. *There is no counter to this argument;* however, it has force only if the American Indian linguistic category that is translated as the Western term "spirit" is equally empty. In the Algonquin-speaking tribes (e.g., Shawnee, Lenni Lenape, Ojibwa, Pottawatomie, and Ottawa), the word translated as "spirit" is "manitou." I propose—perhaps remarkably—that the experiential content of the Native concept *manitou* is closely akin to the experiential content of the Western concept *mind*. And if there are no constructivist qualms about minds, then *manitouki* should not be rejected out of hand, simply because they *seem* to be supernatural by Western lights.[4]

It is not surprising that the American Indian world version has an unjustified reputation for introducing the supernatural into the account of animate beings, for that is the overwhelmingly accepted scholarly and popular interpretation. Notice, for example, how James Howard's (1981) otherwise admirable anthropological treatment of past and present Shawnee culture and ceremony describes a vision quest:

> At the age of puberty or slightly before (about twelve or thirteen years of age), Shawnee boys were sent out into the woods to fast and seek a spirit helper. This spirit helper was a *supernatural creature* who usually appeared to the supplicant in the form of an animal or a bird after the individual had fasted and prayed for a sufficient period. (136; emphasis added)

However, we have seen that there is no distinction between the natural and the supernatural in Native traditions; that a manitou should come during such a ritual is no doubt a very *profound* experience—but it is at the same time utterly *commonplace*. Howard's rather matter-of-fact assumption that a spirit helper is supernatural is wholly the contribution of the standard anthropological interpretation of the ritual, as it tends to be in general when Western interpreters impose their conceptual categories on the American Indian world version.

I have mental experiences, so the predicate "mind" is not empty. Although I do not have direct access to the beliefs and desires, private internal conversations, and secret unspoken aspirations of other human beings—although I cannot directly experience the minds of others—I *know* other human beings have minds.[5] I rehearse the familiar argument if one is required: I exhibit outward behaviors in conjunction with and sometimes caused by my mental events. I grimace when in pain, blush with the occasional lie, and smile when I think of Linda. But I see others exhibiting the same sorts of outward behaviors; others grimace, blush, and smile—they also sing and drum, make love, and wage war. I infer, then, from their outward signs that other human beings have pains, sometimes play fast-and-loose with the truth, and think fondly of their mates just as I do when I behave in similar ways; *I infer from the outward sign that other human beings have minds like I do*. I *know* that you have sentience and volition, desires and beliefs, memories and self-reflection, and the same kind of rich inner mental life that I have.

So, there is pretty good empirical evidence—although not the conclusive evidence demanded by the curmudgeon in the philosophy department—that other human beings have minds. However, if philosophers were honest, they would admit that no argument is really necessary, for the *fact* that others have minds is as deeply ingrained in our world version as the *fact* that there were three red cardinals around my feeder last spring. Indeed, the idea that other human beings could be mindless strikes us as bizarre as the notions that "the three cardinals redded" or "there was red cardinal at the feeder." Minds are both a part of our constructed world—*and what are required to construct that world*.

Now, the traditional Algonquin speaker experiences her own animation—her own *life force*, if you will—so "manitou," like "mind," is not empty.
As an animate being, she eats pemmican and sometimes smokes, shivers in
the cold and sweats in the heat, and has a living body now that will probably die. She directly experiences other human beings eating and smoking,
living and dying, and she infers from their outward signs that they, too, are
animate and have a conscious mental life replete with beliefs and desires.
So she *knows* that other human beings have manitouki as well. But human
beings are not alone in eating and shivering, living and dying; nor are they
alone in exhibiting the kinds of behaviors indicative of animation. Other
things in the world—animal, plant and place, physical force, and cardinal
direction—are *experienced* to be or to act as animate beings; they have manitouki, too. And exactly like the deeply ingrained Western conviction that
other human beings have minds, the notion that such things do not have
manitouki would strike our traditional Algonquin speaker as bizarre—*manitouki are a part of the American Indian constructed world.*

J. Baird Callicott (1989) echoes and embraces our argument from his
own Western philosophical perspective:

> The Indian attitude . . . apparently was based upon the consid-
> eration that since human beings have a physical body and an
> associated consciousness (conceptually hypostatized or reified as
> "spirit"), all other bodily things, animals, plants, and, yes, even
> stones, were also similar in this respect. Indeed, this strikes me
> as an eminently reasonable assumption. I can no more directly
> perceive another human being's consciousness than I can that
> of an animal or plant. I assume that another human being is
> conscious since he or she is perceptibly very like me (in other
> respects) and I am conscious. To anyone not hopelessly preju-
> diced . . . human beings closely resemble in anatomy, physiology,
> and behavior other forms of life. . . . Virtually all things might
> be supposed, without the least strain upon credence, like our-
> selves, to be "alive," that is, conscious, aware, or possessed of
> spirit. (185–86)

Although we agree "in spirit" with Callicott's defense of the "emi-
nently reasonable assumption" that virtually all things might be supposed
to be conscious as we are, he frankly overstates the case. Although the
category *manitou* is fundamental in the Native world version, it is not true
that everything in the grammatical animate class is alive. When Hallowell
asks an Ojibwa informant whether all stones, which are in the animate class,
are living, he replies "No! But *some* are." Hallowell (1960) explains that the

Ojibwa no more believe that all stones are animate than we do, but that their conception of the structure of the world, as well as their confidence in direct experience, force them to leave open the possibility that animate stones will be encountered in the future:

> Whereas we should never expect a stone to manifest animate properties of any kind under any circumstances, the Ojibwa recognize, *a priori*, potentialities for animation in certain classes of objects under certain circumstances. The Ojibwa do not perceive stones, in general, as animate, any more than we do. The crucial test is experience. Is there any personal testimony available? In answer to this question we can say that it is asserted by informants that stones have been seen to move, that some stones manifest other animate properties. (25)

Deloria (1999) concurs, observing that "it is not an article of faith in any Indian religion that everything has spirit," that is, that everything is animate (224). Even so, we see in the Ojibwa informant's cautious response both the kind of reliance on direct experience for verification and the belief about a world that unfixed and unfinished that we have earlier discussed.

Now, it is a commonplace in Native stories and, indeed, in *everyday experience*, that animate beings have an outward form that can change. Iktome, the Spider Person, transformed into a spider and escaped from Iya by scampering down a mouse hole. Calvin Martin (1999) tells the story about an Inupiaq called Katauq, whose spirit went traveling to a great meeting of bowhead whales to learn their habits and ways. Black Elk (2000), as well, conveys a traveling experience when, while touring with Buffalo Bill's show in England, his spirit traveled to Pine Ridge and saw his parents. And everyone has had a dream experience where a friend from afar, or perhaps a loved one who has passed, visits. Although Hallowell mistakenly identifies such metamorphoses as attributes of *persons*—and not of animate beings as we do—he correctly emphasizes "that the capacity for metamorphosis is one of the features which links human beings with the other-than-human [beings] in their behavioral environment . . . Human beings do not differ from them in kind, but in power" (39). Although human beings have the capacity to transform, they may not have the power to do so without the help of other powerful spirit beings.

In the American Indian worldview, then, personhood does not constitute the essence of a human being qua animate being, just as Poole correctly concludes in his analysis of the Western conception of personhood. In general, animate beings are conceived of as they are by the traditional Ojibwa, as having "an inner vital part that is enduring and an outward form which can change. Vital . . . attributes such as sentience, volition, memory, speech are not dependent upon outward appearance but upon the inner vital essence of being" (Hallowell 1960: 42). However, in American Indian traditions an animate being is a *person* by virtue of its membership and participation in an actual network of social and moral relationships and practices with other persons, so moral agency is at the core of a Native conception of persons, just as Poole finds in his analysis of the Western conception of personhood. This means that one cannot be a person in isolation in Native traditions, even with something like Lockean self-reflection or Kantian rationality. However a significant difference from Poole's Western conception is that membership in the network of social and moral relationships goes well beyond the merely human to include many other sorts of nonhuman persons—some very powerful—like Coyote, Iktome, and Iya. Moreover, the relationships one finds in the American Indian community of human and nonhuman persons are closer in nature to kinship relationships (i.e., familial ties), than to the sorts of contractual relationships and obligations between persons one finds in Western accounts of civil society.

Hallowell observes that human and the nonhuman spirit persons participate in the same sorts of familial relationships and practices in his study of the Ojibwa. The Ojibwa share in the widespread American Indian practice of using the kinship term "grandfather" to refer to persons, both human and nonhuman—without any discernable distinction drawn between them—because human and nonhuman grandfathers stand in similar relationships with their human kin. For example, nonhuman persons share their power with human beings by bestowing blessings on them, just as a human grandfather bestows blessings of power through the naming ceremony, in which the elder dreams a child's name. "In other words," says Hallowell (1960), "the relation between a human child and a human grandfather is functionally patterned in the same way as the relation between human beings and grandfathers of an other-than-human class" (22).

So, the Grandfathers (and sometimes *Grandmothers*, for the Shawnee creator Kokumθena is *Our Grandmother*) are powerful nonhuman spirit persons whose intimate familial relationships with human persons are evidenced by the use of the kinship term "grandfather." However, a similar use of other kinship terms indicates that there are other kinds of persons in the nexus of social and moral relationships in the Native world version—in the Native familial social group—besides human persons and the Grandfathers. At the very beginning of Black Elk's (2000) narrative, he shares that his story is "of all life that is holy and is good to tell, and of us two-leggeds sharing in it with the four-leggeds and the wings of the air and all green things; for these are children of one mother and their father is one spirit" (1). Black Elk's conception of nonhuman animals and plants—the "four-leggeds," "wings of the air," and "all green things"—as *siblings* mirrors similar relationships in human families, reinforcing the notion that these other sorts of nonhuman beings also stand in the kinship relationships that constitute personhood. In the human sphere, of course, persons have very special responsibilities arising from their familial connections to parents and siblings—responsibilities that go well beyond the minimal contractual obligations extant in Western civil society. The use of familial kinship terms in conceiving of human relationships with nonhuman animals and plants reinforces the notion that human beings have similar sorts of responsibilities to them as well—to honor and respect the Great Spirit and Mother Earth, and especially their children, as they honor and respect their human family members.[6]

So, human persons participate in a familial social group with other human persons, with powerful spirit persons—Our Grandmother, the Thunderbirds, and Cyclone Person among them—and also with their plant and animal siblings; and it is participation in this actual, concrete nexus of moral relationships and obligations that constitutes their personhood. But other nonhuman entities are members of the Native social group, including the manitouki of the ancestors sometimes experienced in dreams. As well, particular places can have manitouki, when "people live so intimately with environment that they are in relationship to the spirits that live [there]. This is not an article of faith; it is a part of human experience. I think that non-Indians sometimes experience this also when they are in natural environments" (Deloria 1999: 224). Indeed, I have experienced such a presence while visiting the Petroglyph National Monument in New Mexico.

The real meaning of transformation, Calvin Martin suggests, is the kinship of the apparently different sorts of persons in the American Indian familial social group. Animate beings are spirit beings, all of whom have the capacity—if not the power—to change their outward forms. Iktome can transform from human to spider form; Kopit, Old Beaver Person, transforms from human to beaver form; the Three Sisters bring corn, beans, and squash to the Seneca—an then become corn, beans, and squash; White Buffalo Woman transforms into a buffalo after bringing the sacred pipe to the Lakota. The profound lesson is that all animate beings are essentially the same kind of entity—a manitou with a changeable outward form—*so they are all related.*

We are not making a silly claim that what Westerners understand as the natural world is viewed by Indians as "one big family." Kinship groups are fairly small, and relationships within them are close, concrete and directly experienced. Although I might have a contractual sort of obligation not to violate the property rights of every person in a Western civil society, I don't care for every person as I do about kin; the relationships in a civil society are too minimal and too abstract.

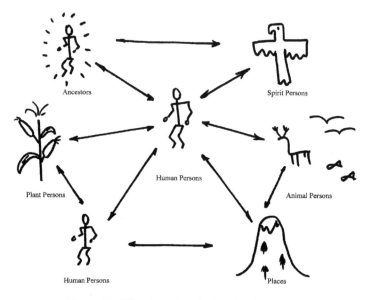

Figure 5.1. The American Indian kinship group

The American Indian kinship group (Figure 5.1), then, has human and nonhuman members of various outward forms, standing in social and moral relationships with other persons, and it is by virtue of these actual, concrete relationships that animate beings are persons. I was taught that *respect for others* grounds these relationships and is the principle moral attitude in the Shawnee tradition; I was taught to "respect every living thing as a person." And Viola Cordova (2004) emphasizes a second important Indian value that undergirds the relationships between persons in the Native familial community—*equality*:

> The Native American recognizes his dependence on the Earth and the Universe. He recognizes no hierarchy of "higher" or "lower" or "simple" or "complex," and certainly not of "primitive" and "modern." Instead of hierarchies he sees *differences* which exist among equal "beings" (mountains, as well as water and air and plants and animals would be included here). The equality is based on the notion, often unstated, that everything that is, is of one process. (177)

That is, all persons in the nexus of relationships have equal value and are due respect by virtue of playing creative roles in the same dynamic process—making and sustaining the American Indian world. We see in the next chapter how *gifting*, the most important normative Native practice, serves to sustain this network of relationships, but Black Elk provides a glimpse. After he and his father kill two deer, Black Elk (2000) felt the moral pangs of having been gifted the deer, but then not being appropriately grateful for the gift or sharing it with other flesh eating nonhuman persons:

> "Father, should we not offer one of these to the wild things?" He looked hard at me again for a while. Then he placed one of the deer with its head to the east, and, facing the west, he raised his hand and cried, "Hey-hey" four times and prayed like this: "Grandfather, the Great Spirit, behold me! To all the wild things that eat flesh, this I have offered that my people may live and the children grow up with plenty." (64–65)

Notably, sharing the gift of the deer with "all the wild things that eat flesh"—gifting to them—helps to ensure that the Lakota will have plenty—unsurprising, because "we are all related."[7] *And it should not escape our attention that Coyote's error in our story was violating this most fundamental of Native moral practices!*

An American Indian Expansive Conception of Persons

We began with Poole's insightful critique of a prominent Western conception of persons, finding that in our development of an American Indian conception we could agree that personhood is not what is essential to being human. Human beings are, instead, "spirit beings"—manitouki—who just happen to have a human form. We agreed as well that human beings become persons—and sustain their identity as persons—by virtue of their participation social and moral relationships with other persons. In the Native worldview, the relationships and obligations that engender and sustain persons are familial in nature and are based on respect and equality, so they are moral relationships. Thus, moral agency is at the core of the Indian conception of personhood.

Unlike Poole's analysis of the Western notion of persons, however, we saw that the Native conception is *expansive*, for all sorts of nonhuman spirit beings—ancestors and animals, plants and places, physical forces and cardinal directions, the Sun, Earth, and other powerful *manitouki*—are members of the American Indian kinship group, and so are persons.

Although there are nonhuman animal and plant persons in Native traditions, not all animate beings are persons, for the standards for personhood are pretty high—one must participate in a social nexus more akin to a family than a civil society. More generally, not everything that is in the grammatically animate class of things is a person, although it is fair to say that being animate is a necessary condition for personhood. But for that matter, not all human beings are persons on most Western accounts. Indeed, I would argue that not all human beings are persons on the American Indian account as well. I imagine that cultural anthropologists Hallowell observing the Ojibwa and Howard the Shawnee never became a part of the familial Native groups they were studying; that would have negatively influenced the kind of objectivity required for a proper scientific investigation. I doubt that they performed the requisite ceremonies and participated in the life of the tribe in the way that would make them *real persons*.

I close with a story recounted by Lee Hester of the visit of John Proctor—the oldest living Creek medicine man—to a class Hester was teaching entitled "Native American Identity." In response to a student's question, "What makes you Creek?," Mr. Proctor replied, "If you come to the stomp ground for four years, take the medicines and dance the dances, then you are Creek" (Cheney and Hester 2001: 327). This seemingly simple and straightforward response masks a quite profound notion: Becoming Creek—becoming a *real* person—requires taking the medicines and dancing the dances; one must perform the ceremonies, assume the tribal roles and participate in the Creek life and familial social group to be a person.

6

The Semantic Potency
of Performance

This chapter exp____es the third common theme in American Indian world versions, the sem___ic potency of performance. Through a consideration of various sorts of sp___ch acts, dance, a naming ceremony, and Native gifting traditions, the ch___ers shows how *performing with a symbol* empowers the symbol, transform___e participants, categorizes and orders experiences, and helps construct th___American Indian world.

Opening Reflections and
R___ninders About Performances

We ended our co___deration of the American Indian expansive concep-tion of persons wi___Lee Hester's story about Creek medicine man John Proctor's visit to hi___ass on Native identity. Mr. Proctor told the class that one is Creek after ___ning to the stomp grounds for four years, taking the medicines, and dan___g the dances. This is a deceptively simple response; to come to the gro___ds, take the medicines, and dance means that one must participate in ___e Creek social and ceremonial life to be Creek. One must participate in t___se performances and practices that sustain both social relationships and rel___ous ceremonies. In my own experience, coming to the Shawnee grounds is not just showing up; coming means very long travel, reconnecting with clan brothers and sisters, receiving counsel from elders, listening to the stories, sharing the evening feast, remembering those who have passed—and then there's the raffle. More importantly, coming to cer-emony means participating in purifications and prayers, in the ritual ball and hoop games, and sometimes even in the dance. Like being Creek, being Shawnee means taking the medicines and dancing the dances—one must perform the ceremonies.

Now, the notion that participation in ceremony—playing a part in ritual *performance*—is important to being Creek or Shawnee should not be such a foreign notion; indeed, many a bride and groom have participated in a wedding ceremony with profound *ontological* consequences; the ceremony transforms its participants and empowers its symbols—the vows and rings among them. Likewise, Native ceremonies and performances are transforma-tive and empowering; taking the medicines and dancing the dances have the power to make one Creek or Shawnee. More generally, performances have the power to categorize and order, or recategorize and reorder—in short, *create* and *recreate*—the American Indian world. In American Indian traditions, the action, procedure, or performance is the principal vehicle of meaning and the way by which the world is made.

Constructivism embraces the idea that performances can contribute to the creation and re-creation of worlds. The view that linguistic versions of the world—statements, theories, and models—make worlds by identifying, categorizing, and ordering sense experiences has been a commonplace for us, ever since our earlier discussion of Goodman's constructivism. However, we have focused almost exclusively on linguistic versions of the world that are supposed to be literal and descriptive; yet, nonlinguistic and nondeno-tational versions are no less important in the making of an actual world. Music, painting, poetry, dance, and other sorts of performative endeavors can categorize and order experiences and reorganize existing kinds in ways little different from linguistic literal versions of the world.

A straightforward exercise easily demonstrates how relatively simple yet fundamental actions, procedures, or performances categorize and order our world of experiences. Give someone a bag of "odds and ends"—objects of various sizes, colors, shapes, weights, compositions, values, and so on— and then ask that the objects be *sorted* without specifying criteria for the sort. Sorters will invent their own criteria—their own categories—and sort in accordance with those criteria. They have, then, organized the world through their sorting activity—here a pile of blue objects, there a pile of red; here a pile of organic objects, there a pile of inorganic objects. Sorting activity imposes an order and *creates* facts—"the blue pile is in a different location than the red pile" and "the blue and inorganic piles have common members." It should not concern us, by the way, whether sorters carry out the task by specifying a predicate, say, "x is blue" or "x is inorganic," or whether their sorting is a nonlinguistic activity, for certainly there are "sorts of both sorts." No doubt, specifying a predicate is an important way to sort for people with a mature command of language—perhaps even the princi-pal way mature sorters sort. But research in early childhood development indicates that prelinguistic children engage in rudimentary sorting activities, and so impose an order on their experiences (Sigel 1983).

In Chapter 3, I discussed how collecting is an activity by which we construct facts. In this chapter, I reiterate that collecting is a fundamental kind of activity—indeed, as fundamental as sorting—but I also observe that collecting and sorting are different kinds of activities. Sorting compares objects, but it does not involve viewing a sorted pile as a collection with a cardinality. Sorters ask, "How are these alike or different?" while collectors merely view an aggregate of objects as a collection. Again, specifying a predicate is an important way to collect for people with mature linguistic skills—as it is for sorting—but there is evidence that prelinguistic children collect[1] (Wynn 1990, 1992a, 1992b).

Although sorting and collecting are two of the most fundamental world-constructing activities, more complex actions, procedures, and performances also categorize and organize experiences. In subsequent sections, I consider speech acts—prayers or storytellings, counselings, or healings—as such world-constructing performances. Then, keeping in mind that there are no sharp distinctions between various kinds of performances in Native traditions, I examine how Native dance, naming, and gifting ceremonies and performances not only organize and reinforce social and moral relationships in the Indian world, but make an Indian world.

Before proceeding, it is important to remember that actions, procedures, and performances are central to the accounts of truth, verification, and knowledge in American Indian traditions. Recalling that the *respectful* success in achieving any lesser goal is informed by the primary overarching Native goal—walking the right road—where all of our actions and performances are mindful of our proper place in the network of relationships with other human and nonhuman persons, we proposed that an action or performance is true for a subject just in case it is respectfully successful in achieving a goal. As before, such actions and performances can be storytellings and other speech acts, healings, ceremonial dances, or simply observing the world to construct connections between entities or events. Moreover, an action or performance is justified for a subject just in case the subject has directly experienced the respectful success of the performance, or the respectful success is endorsed by tradition. Finally, we saw that knowledge in Native traditions is principally procedural knowledge that is closely tied to concrete, direct experience: A subject knows how to perform to achieve a goal just in case the performance is true and justified for the subject.

Symbols and Their Performance

I reiterate my debt to Sam Gill's (1982, 1987) fundamental insight that understanding American Indian religion in particular—and the Native world version in general—depends on the recognition that the Native linguistic tradition is oral, not written.[2] Unlike Western communication, where the written text is ubiquitous to the point of invisibility, *performance* of or with all sorts of unwritten symbols becomes the principal vehicle of meaning—and world creation and recreation—in American Indian traditions. "[T]he significance of Native American religious symbols is not something we can determine by isolating and decoding particular symbols," Gill concludes. "[T]hey are inseparable from the performance of which they are a part" (1982: 61).

The function of a symbol is the same in Western and American Indian traditions. Whether a national flag, a wedding ring, the written text of the Gettysburg Address, a Dine sand painting, the Lakota pipe, or a Native dream or vision experience—all symbolic entities—a symbol is something that stands for or denotes something else. Here Black Elk (2000) tells John Neihardt of the symbolism of the Lakota pipe:

> These four ribbons hanging here on the stem are the four quarters of the universe. The black one is for the west where the thunder beings live to send us rain; the white one for the north, whence comes the great cleansing wind; the red one for the east, whence springs the light and where the morning star lives to give men wisdom; the yellow for the south, whence come the summer and the power to grow.
>
> But these four spirits are only one Spirit after all, and this eagle feather here is for that One, which is like a father, and also it is for the thoughts of men that should rise high as eagles do. Is not the sky a father and the earth a mother, and are not all living things with feet or wings or roots their children? And this hide upon the mouthpiece here, which should be bison hide, is for the earth, from whence we came and at whose breast we suck as babies all our lives, along with all the animals and birds and trees and grasses. And because it means all this, and more than any man can understand, the pipe is holy. (2)

But although a symbol can be meaningful—be it the Lakota pipe or a wedding ring—the symbol is largely impotent unless it is performed—and this insight is at the heart of the semantic potency of performance. Consider that the wedding ring in the jeweler's case is certainly symbolic, as is the text of a traditional wedding vow. Yet neither of them have any power until they play a part in a wedding ceremony, that is, until there is a performance with them. The acts of speaking the vow and giving the ring during the ceremony empower the symbols and effect a transformation of the participants—and the creation of all sorts of new relationships and obligations. Likewise, the Lakota pipe is symbolic, but it is not fully potent until it is used in performance in the offering ceremony, and the power of a Dine sand painting is not realized until it is used in a healing (Gill 1982: 62–66). Finally, Black Elk describes his symbolic dog vision in great detail, but its power is not unleashed until it is performed as a heyoka ceremony.

The performance with a symbol imbues the symbol with power, but there are other related and interconnected influences and results. Performances with symbols can create and reinforce social and moral relationships—as in the Western performance with wedding vows and rings—and in the Native performance of gifting, which is explored later. A performance can enhance or reaffirm the significance of a symbol itself, as when the entire stadium rises to the flag and sings the national anthem. Goals can be achieved by the performance with a symbol, as in Dine sand painting cures or ceremonies to restore balance or equilibrium in the world or in the People; and Black Elk (2000) reminds that "a man who has a vision is not able to use the power of it until after he has performed the vision on earth for the people to see," so unleashing the power of the symbol can itself be a goal achieved (157). A performance with a symbol can enhance one's emotional understanding, as when a mourner touches the flag-draped coffin of his father during the funeral ceremony. And, finally, all logic professors hope—if not believe—that performances with symbols can enhance conceptual understanding in their students.

Perhaps the most profound and fundamental American Indian world creating performance is the speech act in its many forms, including saying prayers and singing sacred songs, and especially telling stories.[3] Indeed, it would be fair to say that a speech act plays a central role in almost all other Native performances and ceremonies. In the speech act, one performs with meaningful symbols—words, of course—but the performance of the words in ceremony empowers them and is transformative. The text of the Gettysburg Address is certainly meaningful; but only when performed in the dedication ceremony of the battlefield did the words have the power to sanctify and transform the place into a sacred site. Likewise, Native prayers, songs, and stories have meaning when unperformed—that is how people outside of the tradition come to know them (i.e., as written texts). Consider that the text of Black Road's prayer—as the text of Lincoln's Address—is indeed meaningful:

> Grandfathers, you where the sun goes down, you of the sacred wind where the white giant lives, you where the day comes forth and the morning star, you where lives the power to grow, you of the sky and you of the earth, wings of the air and four-leggeds of the world, behold! I, myself, with my horse nation have done what I was to do on earth. To all of you I offer this pipe that my people may live! (Black Elk 2000: 134)

However, when spoken in ceremony as a part of the performance of the horse dance, when the sacred pipe was offered to the Powers of the World, then the prayer empowers the symbol—the pipe—and reaffirms the Lakota world version. Relationships between human persons and powerful non-human spirit persons—the Grandfathers—are re-established, and bonds between human persons and their winged and four-legged brothers are reaffirmed, thus reminding both the Powers and the People, "we are all relatives." Also, in offering the pipe to the four cardinal directions, to the sky and to the earth, the performance conveys the centrality of place in the Lakota world version. Finally, and importantly, the performance of offering the pipe is a gifting to the Powers of the World that creates reciprocal obligations—in return for the gift of the offering, the Powers, who stand in a network of social and moral relationships with human persons, are obligated to care for the Lakota in return. "To all of you I offer this pipe that my people may live!"

We earlier visited Ohiyesa's account of an exchange of origin stories between a Western missionary and a group of Indians to suggest a difference between the function of origin stories in each tradition. We proposed then that the missionary's conviction that his Judeo-Christian origin story corresponds to fact is different from the Native notion that the successful telling of an origin story puts the People's experiences into perspective and helps them to understand their place in the world, that the performance is the vehicle for traditional knowledge and moral values, and that a story strengthens tribal bonds and ties to other human and nonhuman persons in the world. These and related purposes are to be achieved by the other stories we have considered. The Menominee story of the "The Man Who Loved the Frog Songs" teaches the consequences of forgetting that we are all related and acting on a disrespectful and selfish desire to learn something from others without permission. "How Buzzard Got His Clothing" teaches the Seneca the consequences of a selfish pride, and the Lakota "Coyote, Iktome, and the Rock" teaches the consequences of gifting falsely. It should be clear, however, that the *written* text of stories cannot put experiences into perspective, teach moral lessons and strengthen tribal bonds in an oral tradition. The stories must be performed.

Irving Hallowell discusses Ojibwa sacred stories, emphasizing that the characters in their ritualized, seasonally restricted narrations—their performances—are regarded as living, powerful nonhuman persons who stand in social and moral relationships with their human relatives. However, Hallowell (1960) misinterprets an observation made by William Jones (1905) that "[m]yths are thought of as conscious beings, with powers of thought and action" as a statement about the characters in the myth—and not about the sacred stories, themselves (27). But this, I maintain, is exactly what Jones meant; and a similar observation is made by Calvin Martin (1999) about the Inupiaq conception of story, that a story is an animate entity with a "yua"—a spirit. Indeed, after telling a story about an Inupiaq man, Katauq, who goes traveling to learn the ways of bowhead whales, Martin remarks that it would not be unusual for the Inupiaq to regard the story as thinking about them. But a lifeless written text—like a lifeless corpse—is not a conscious being with powers of thought and action; a story is enlivened and empowered, animated and transformative through its performance. And oral events like storytellings are spiritual entities that give shape and meaning, and create beauty and orderliness in the world (Gill 1982: 39). In short, the performance of Native stories contributes to the construction of an American Indian world.

Dance is another powerful world creating performance with symbols in Native traditions. We have already seen that the Black Elk narrative is replete with accounts of the many dances the holy man saw in visions—as well as their performance before the people to empower them—and the resulting world-makings. I know something more about dance in the Shawnee tradition, and I say something about it, but no more that one could find in James Howard's (1981) account of Shawnee ceremonialism. Although there are some differences in the ceremonial cycles of the various Shawnee bands, the spring and fall Bread Dances, as well as the Green Corn ceremony, constitute the heart of the yearly ritual cycle. The Bread Dances offer thanks to the Creator for agricultural and hunting bounty, and reaffirm the duality of woman as cultivator and man as hunter, with the spring Bread Dance celebrating the traditional role of woman and the fall Bread Dance celebrating the traditional role of man. Corn bread—tami takwaa—figures prominently in the ceremony. "The Bread Dance," observes Howard, "thus serves to dramatize the complementary roles of men and women in the Shawnee economic pattern and in this way reinforces group mores. The Green Corn," he continues, "seems to be essentially a junior version of the Bread Dance," with other agricultural produce besides corn bread prominently displayed (224–25).

Although not an inaccurate empirical description of the ceremony, the Western cultural anthropologist Howard's portrayal misses what is really important about Shawnee dances. The ceremony in all its aspects—the drumming and rattling, singing and dancing—is an animated entity with a spirit created by the participants. The ceremony not only affirms the traditional roles of man and woman, but it celebrates, values, and perpetuates those roles. The dancers are responsible for the prosperity of the entire nation; and, having once danced, I can convey that it is quite a solemn responsibility for the participants. The dance is a gift of thankfulness to the Creator and so creates the kinds of relationships and obligations characteristic of gift exchanges in gifting traditions. Perhaps most important, the dance empowers its symbols—the drum, the song, and the bread—and transforms its participants and the world.

Another account of Shawnee dance told to Trowbridge by Tenskwatawa illustrates its power to transform. Tenskwatawa tells of an ancient group called "the juggling society," all of whose members had been dead for about one hundred years at the time of Trowbridge's 1824 interview. According to Tenskwatawa, admission to the secret society involved the clubbing and dismemberment of young initiates, then feeding their mangled limbs to the dogs. After the old men sang powerful ritual songs, the initiate's head was placed on a bed of leaves and the dogs vomited what they had eaten.

> This mass was covered with leaves, the society danced around the bed to the right, four times in quick succession, during which the oldest men sung very violently, and at the end of the dance they seated themselves; and the boy, having exactly the appearance which he had before being killed, arose & took his place among the members. (Kinietz and Voegelin 1939: 36)

Whether Tenskwatawa expected Trowbridge to understand literally or figuratively his account of the society is largely irrelevant to the more important point that the dance—in conjunction with the passionately performed song—was regarded as an extremely powerful and transformative ritual.

The Shawnee Naming Ceremony

Naming ceremonies are a commonplace in American Indian traditions, and naming provides another fine example of how a performance with a symbol is empowering and transformative, and categorizes and orders the Native world. And although our discussion focuses on the traditional Shawnee naming ceremony, we may confidently extend our most fundamental ontological observations to other American Indian traditions.

The Shawnee nation is first of all divided into five major political divisions or *septs*, each traditionally responsible for various tribal duties: the Chalaakaaθa (Chillicothe) and the θawikila, the septs from which the principal peace chief is chosen; the Mekoche, the keepers of the medicine; the war sept, the Kishpoko, from which the war chief is chosen; and the Pekowi, the sept that traditionally furnishes the speaker for the tribal chief (Howard 1981: 25–30). The name groups that are our focus, the *um'somaki*, are found in each of these political divisions.

Voegelin (Voegelin & Voegelin 1935) records six Shawnee name groups representing various kinds or characteristics of nonhuman animals: *Turkey um'soma* representing bird life;[4] *Turtle um'soma* representing aquatic life; *Rounded-feet um'soma* representing carnivorous animals like the wolf; *Horse um'soma* representing herbivorous animals like the deer; *Raccoon um'soma* representing "animals having paws which can scratch like those of the raccoon and bear"; and *Rabbit um'soma* representing a gentle temperament (617). Alford (1936) concurs that the name groups are six in number (3n); however, Tenskwatawa shared that the Shawnee anciently had thirty-four "tribes," but there were twelve at the time of his 1824 interview with Trowbridge[5] (Kinietz and Voegelin: 16–17). "In the abstract," Voegelin (Voegelin & Voegelin 1935) proposes, "the number of name groups is often said to be twelve, but no more than six are ever specified" (622). At least one contemporary band has thirteen *um'somaki*. Howard (1981) notes that a Shawnee's *um'soma* is not a totem in a "strict sense," and that there are restrictions neither on the hunting nor eating of one's name group animal (94).

Traditionally, tribal members belonged to a name group by virtue of a naming ceremony and not by descent. Voegelin (Voegelin & Voegelin 1935) describes one such ceremony practiced by the Kishpoko and Pekowi septs. The father of a child to be named asks two elders to come to the house on the evening of the ninth day after the child's birth. The elders need not be family relatives, nor members of the same *um'soma* as either parent; however, it is unlikely that elders will be asked to be name-givers if several of their own children have died. The father asks the elders to

> study about this matter over and over; think about the animals [connected to the name groups]—how they act, how they move, everything like that. . . . When you go to sleep, keep this thought with you; maybe you'll dream about that name, some way. If you don't dream about it, maybe you'll just think about it, and so find a good name. (Billy Williams, quoted by Voegelin & Voegelin 1935: 622–23)

After the appropriate prayers are offered to the Creator and a name occurs to each elder, they must determine to which *um'soma* the name belongs. Voegelin conveys that parents usually request that the child be a member of one of their name groups; however, if both parents are "sickly," or if they make no specific request, then the child is commonly named into name-giver's *um'soma* (624). According to Alford (1936), however, the child is "automatically" named into the name-giver's *um'soma* (3n).

On the morning of the tenth day, the naming ceremony takes place before assembled family and friends. Each elder in turn presents the name he or she has found, and describes the characteristics and habits of the animal represented by the name's *um'soma*. The parents then choose the name "which sounds good," and the father announces the choice. The child is handed to the name-giver, who offers a lengthy prayer to the Creator, noting that the Creator gave the animals power and wisdom, and put them on earth to "carry us to be a man or a woman some day." Then, after repeating the name four times, the name-giver places a string of white, finely cut beads around the child's neck, to be worn until the string breaks. The assembled family and friends then greet the newly named person and breakfast together (Billy Williams, recorded by Voegelin & Voegelin 1935: 622–23).

Now, Voegelin (Voegelin & Voegelin 1935) proposes that the *um'somaki* "function primarily as friendship groups in which all the members of the group have the privilege of boasting about the animals associated with their own name group and belittling those pertaining to other name groups" (628). Alford (1936) similarly observes that the *um'somaki* are "a kind of social clanship" and engender "strong partisanship and much pleasant rivalry among the Shawnees" (4). I believe, however, that these analyses underplay the more fundamental ontological function of a person's *um'soma* and the naming ceremony that bestows it.

A name—when well and wisely chosen—is an animate entity that takes care of its bearer; if not, the bearer of the name might be "sickly" or have other sorts of evils befall her or him, in which case the person may need to be renamed after the original name is ritually removed. A good name cares for its bearer, and the person comes to have characteristics associated with the kind of animal represented by the *um'soma* (Voegelin & Voegelin 1935: 626). So, for example, Turtle people are very good swimmers—but trust me, they are slow; Turkey people, on the other hand, are ever vigilant and ready to take wing at a moment's notice—my kind of folks. Voegelin conveys as well that there is an "emotional rapport" between persons and the animals their *um'soma* represents, and that various advantages and obligations arise from the name bearer's association with them (628). And sometimes the *um'soma* animals give aid to their human kin; but why not, since we are all related?

The point for our present purposes should be clear because we are exploring the significance and potency of ceremony—of performance with a symbol—in American Indian traditions. The dreaming of the name by the elders in the Shawnee tradition—found after solemn deliberation and prayer to the Creator—and its performance in the naming ceremony create a bond between the name and its bearer, giving the name the power to care for and transform its bearer; he or she acquires some of the characteristics of, and emotional bonds and moral obligations to the *um'soma* animal. Moreover, the ceremony contributes to an ongoing categorization and ordering of human and nonhuman persons into the kinds represented by the Turkeys and Turtles, Rounded-foot and Raccoon, Horse and Rabbit. In the human world, one's *um'soma* is the source of lifelong friendships and good-natured rivalries, and was a traditional determinant of certain tribal roles and responsibilities. Consider, for example, that only a Turkey or Turtle man may keep the Kishpoko sept's sacred bundle. Moreover, because of the fecundity of egg-laying creatures, the leader of the cooks and hunters at the spring Bread Dance must be either a Turkey or Turtle. Finally, a Rabbit person is ideal as the principal chief because the role is essential a peaceful one (Howard 1981: 94–97). The Shawnee naming ceremony, then, is a powerful and transformative performance that creates and recreates the Shawnee world.

Gifting as a World-Constructing Performance

William Penn was one of the earliest Europeans to treat with the Leni Lenape and the Shawnee in 1682. He mused about the Natives' demeanor and behavior—especially with respect to material wealth and property—in a 1683 letter to the Committee of the Free Society of Traders in London:

> But in liberality they excel, nothing is too good to set for a friend; give them a fine gun, coat, or other thing, it may pass twenty hands before it sticks; light of heart, strong affections, but soon spent. The most merry creatures that live; they feast and dance perpetually, almost; they never have much, nor want much; wealth circulateth like the blood, all parties partake, and none shall want what another hath, yet exact observers of property.[6] (Penn, quoted in Harvey 1855: 15)

Now, coming from an economic and social system wherein barter between individuals was the primary means of exchanging material goods, the "liberality" of the Shawnee—evidenced by the passing of material objects from hand-to-hand, and wealth circulating like blood—must have seemed rather odd. However, we will see that Penn was witness to the kinds of behaviors characteristic of an economic and social system wherein the *gift* is the primary means of exchange. We will also see that in American Indian traditions gifting is yet another performance with a symbol that is empowering and transformative, and that serves to categorize and order the world.

It will be both useful and instructive to compare Native gifting traditions with an influential—if not the prominent—Western conception of civil society as developed by John Locke in the *Second Treatise on Civil Government*.[7] It will be useful, because the differences between Native traditions that consider the gift as the most important means of exchange and other societies based upon barter—as is Locke's, Penn's, and *ours*—emerge in sharp relief. And it will be instructive, because it teaches something about gifting practices in contemporary liberal societies that adopt Lockean assumptions about human beings and property.

According to Locke's seventeenth-century European conception of the law of reason—the law of nature—human beings are "naturally" individuals with inherent rights to life, liberty, and property. The sole and proper ends of a government created by the mutual consent of free, equal individuals are the regulation and protection of their property and the defense of the commonwealth from "foreign injury." Finally, an assumption that is important for our analysis: the principal mode of exchange between individuals in the Lockean scheme is barter—the impersonal exchange of property for property. In fact, gifting as a mode of exchange is almost never considered in the *Second Treatise*.

Locke begins his well-known story about the origin of civil society by employing a device commonly used by modern period political philosophers, the *state of nature*, a fictional condition in which human beings find themselves prior to and outside of civil society. In this condition, independent individuals are in a state of perfect freedom and equality, and they may do what they will with their persons and property in order to preserve themselves and their possessions. This liberty and equality is guaranteed by the *law of nature*, which further grounds the rather minimal fundamental moral obligation that individuals in the state of nature have to each other: "no one ought to harm another in his life, health, liberty or possessions" (Locke 1986: 9). But because of the difficulties in knowing and executing the law of nature, as well as the general insecurity of life and property in the state of nature, individuals freely quit the natural state by entering into a compact with others of like mind to unite into a community for comfort, protection and to secure their property. Thus, through the mutual consent of free, equal, and independent individuals, civil society—and the authority to govern it—is created (71).

Important to our comparison of Native gifting traditions with societies based on barter are the origin, nature, and exchange of property. In the beginning, according to Locke, God gave the world to humanity in common—as well as reason, so that humanity could make the best use of the world to preserve itself. However, although the world is held in common, there must be some way that particular individuals may lay claim to some portion of the common stock for personal use, as Locke illustrates by an appeal to "the wild Indian": "The fruit or venison which nourishes the wild Indian, who knows no enclosure, and is still a tenant in common, must be his, and so his—i.e., a part of him, that another can no longer have any right to it before it can do him any good for the support of his life" (19).

One lays claim to portions of the common stock through labor. When I collect the basket of plums from the unclaimed tree given to all in common, then they become my property by virtue of my picking them (20). However, the law of nature also places a limit on property: One may own only as much as one can use before it spoils, for to take more from what is held in common than one can use is tantamount to robbery—this individual is "invading his neighbor's share" (25).

Thus, if I gather one hundred bushels of plums—more than I can possibly use before some spoil—I've violated the law of nature, and so should be punished as a transgressor. However, if I can *barter* some of my plums for something a bit more permanent, say, for nuts, then nothing has perished needlessly, and I have not violated the rights of others by taking what they have a right to from the common stock. It would be even better were I to barter some of my plums for "a piece of metal, . . . shells, . . . a sparkling pebble or a diamond," for these things do not perish. And because they do not perish, one may heap up as much of them as one desires (29). Such is Locke's account of the origin and utility of money and estates.

Locke's discussion of the Earth as property is particularly interesting—and telling. Just like other things given to humanity in common, the Earth itself is part of the common stock, and so, becomes one's property through labor: "As much land as a man tills, plants, improves, cultivates, and can use the product of, so much is his property" (22). Humanity was commanded by God to subdue the Earth, that is, to improve it for the benefit of human beings—for it needs improvement, given that "Nature and the earth furnished only the almost worthless materials as in themselves" (28). Indeed, "of the products of the earth useful to the life of man, nine-tenths are the effects of labour" (26). And, as in the earlier case of my plums, if I occupy more land than I can use—my grain or grass rots in the field—then I violate the "spoilage clause" of law of nature.

Moreover, Locke considers land left unimproved as waste, "land that is left wholly to nature, that hath no improvement of pasturage, tillage, or planting, is called, as indeed it is, waste: and we shall find the benefit of it amount to little more than nothing" (27), which motivates his implicit invitation to take the land in the Americas, because it remains unimproved and wasted:

yet there are still great tracts of ground to be found, which the
inhabitants thereof, not having joined with the rest of mankind
in the consent of the use of their common money, lie waste, and
are more than the people who dwell on it, do, or can make use
of, and so still lie in common. (29)

Granting that barter is the principal means of exchange in Lockean
liberal societies does not imply, of course, that the gift is wholly absent as
a means of exchange. However, the nature of gift giving is influenced by
the liberal assumptions that human beings are free and equal individuals
who incur obligations when they enter into contractual agreements with or
promises to others, but not otherwise. So, if you invite me to your birthday
party and I arrive without a gift in hand, then I have acted rudely—but I
have not acted immorally. This is because an actual gift must be personally
and voluntarily bestowed; imposing any sort of moral obligation to give a
gift is tantamount to coercion, hence the action is not the giving of a gift.
According to Maurice Godelier, it's an exchange more akin to taxation or
extortion (1999: 14).

It is somehow fitting that we juxtapose Locke's classic development of
liberalism with another classic, Marcel Mauss's (2000) anthropological study
of gifting economies called *The Gift*, first published in 1950. Indeed, it is all
the more fitting, since Mauss is a staunch critic of liberal political theory—as
well as utilitarian moral theory—because both assume an impoverished conception of human beings as essentially independent, free, and self-interested
individuals, ignoring that they are essentially social beings. We have already
seen how this assumption lies at the heart of Lockean liberalism: Human
beings are free, equal, and rights-bearing individuals who enter into or quit
civil society by giving or revoking their consent. Likewise, in making the
criterion of right action the maximization of nonmoral good—pleasure or
whatever—for the greatest number of people, utilitarianism understands the
pleasure or pain of *individual* human beings as values in a calculus. The moral
right is the collective *individual* good.

In contrast, Mauss meets head-on the Lockean notion of a state of
nature existing outside of Western liberal civil society wherein *individuals*
exchanged useful *material wealth* by way of *simple barter*.[8] Instead, after a
study of existing indigenous societies—including the Tlingit and Haida in
Alaska, and Melanesian and Polynesian peoples—as well as an interpretation of ancient economies, Mauss concludes that such a Lockean "natural
economy" never existed. It is first of all not individuals, but groups of various sorts—families, clans, tribes, and so on—that impose and incur obligations of and through exchange in the indigenous societies he considers.
Second, exchanges are not the simple barter of plums for nuts or nuts for a

piece of metal, that is, they are not a mere trade of useful material objects. Instead, objects of exchange include immaterial objects and events such as dances and festival, rituals and banquets—and sometimes women and children—and they are acts of politeness that create and reinforce relationships and obligations. Finally, in indigenous societies gifting is the primary mode of exchange; but the voluntary nature of its Western counterpart is absent. Mauss (2000) found that gifting in indigenous societies may appear at times to be voluntary, but in reality it creates all sorts of obligations the fulfillment of which "are strictly compulsory, on pain of private or public warfare"[9] (5–6).

In fact, Mauss identifies three distinct obligations incurred by the gift in various indigenous societies, namely, to give, accept, and reciprocate, evidenced in part by gifting practices in the Maori tradition, and it is the *source* of the obligations that is of particular interest. Mauss concludes that one incurs an obligation to reciprocate when one receives a gift or present "because to accept something from somebody is to accept some part of his spiritual essence, of his soul" (12). Thus, a gift is a symbol enlivened by—animated by—the gifting performance; one receives a part of the giver, and one must return that which is an essential part of the giver. Failing to discharge this obligation is against Maori law and morality, but it is also dangerous, for gifts, presents, and ritual or communal acts "all exert a magical or religious hold" over the recipient (12). The gift—which is itself enlivened and aware—"seeks to return to . . . its 'place of origin' or to produce, on behalf of the clan and the native soil from which it sprang, an equivalent to replace it" (13). Mauss speculates that the obligations to give and to accept are no less compelling in the Maori tradition, for refusing either to give or accept is a rejection of relatedness—of "alliance and commonality"—and is "tantamount to declaring war" (13).

Mauss identifies similar obligations to give, accept, and reciprocate a gifting in the potlatch festivals—rituals of competitive, antagonistic, and extravagant giving, consumption and, sometimes, destruction of wealth—practiced by the Alaskan Tlingit and Haida. Honor and the saving of face apparently play pivotal roles in this gifting practice. One's position or rank as clan chief or noble is first of all dependent on fulfilling the obligations to both give and attend potlatches. One must give potlatches for family members—both living and passed—because one's hierarchical tribal position requires good fortune and the favor of ancestors, and one evidences good fortune and favor through the extravagant consumption and sharing of wealth. On the other hand, one loses face, rank, and honor by failing to fulfill the obligation to give the potlatch. Likewise, face and honor suffer if one refuses to attend a potlatch—or rejects a gift in general—for doing so indicates that one is unable to reciprocate a present or a potlatch gift.

This implies, of course, that the obligation to reciprocate a giving—most of the time with interest—is the core *moral* obligation. Indeed, Mauss reports that failure to reciprocate a gifting in Tlingit and Haida traditions, or to destroy one's wealth to match the sacrifice of another, means losing one's face "forever" (33–42).

Some of the most important objects of distribution and destruction in Alaskan Native potlatch rituals are sacred copper emblazoned items, universally regarded amongst the tribes as *animate objects*. Mauss conveys that despite the histories and fortunes of the potlatch—whether they are exchanged or destroyed—these objects have names and individuality, and permanent and perpetual value. They have the power to attract wealth, honor and alliances, and to demand their own distribution or destruction. But, in fact, maintaining honor and rank, alliances and face sometimes obligates one to distribute or destroy, return in kind or consume these animate, sacred objects of economic and "magical" value (44–46).

From his study of Polynesian, Melanesian, and Alaskan indigenous societies, Mauss draws general conclusions. First, he holds that the principal, if not the sole form of exchange in indigenous societies is the gift exchange of material goods and nonmaterial events and services—with all of the attending obligations to give, accept, and reciprocate—between various familial groups, instead of a barter exchange of material goods between free, independent, and equal individuals. Second, these obligations are grounded in the notion that the gift is an animate being that is enlivened or ensouled, and imbued with various powers and values—especially with powers to punish transgressions of the moral obligations to give, accept, and reciprocate the gift. A final important finding—one Mauss fails to fully explore, I think—is that gifting performances and practices in indigenous traditions promote and preserve equilibrium (14, 46).

There is much to applaud in Mauss's study of indigenous traditions, despite the fact that he embraces the false and unfortunate view that such societies are archaic and primitive antecedents of modern civilized Western society. First of all, his critique of Lockean liberalism is on the mark, especially his debunking of the dubious *state of nature* wherein free, independent, and equal human beings with the full panoply of rights to property bartered material goods. Human beings in such a "natural state" have never existed. By the way, the Western tradition's fiction that human beings are essentially independent and free individuals has cost dearly both human and nonhuman beings alike.

Once more, Mauss correctly discovers that gifting with its attending obligations, and not bartering, is the primary means of exchange in indigenous traditions—something Locke never entertains. Well, Locke *almost* never entertains the gift. Indeed, we saw that Locke does begin his account of property with the *gift* of the world to humanity in common from God in the *Second Treatise*. Yet, even if we take Locke seriously in his assertion that the Deity gifted the world to human beings, this is clearly different from a gifting in the Native sense, for Locke says nothing about humanity's obligation to reciprocate. Locke isn't even particularly gracious in acknowledging the gift on behalf of humanity; the gift from God is largely worthless until human beings labor on it. Nor is the gift intended to create, preserve, and reproduce social relationships—as is the purpose of indigenous acts of gifting. Indeed, what social relationships exist to be preserved and reproduced by gifting between God and humanity, humanity and the world, or even human being to human being? None: In the state of nature, the minimal negative social relationships that exist—do not harm the lives or possessions of others—are created and reproduced by reason and preserved by individuals empowered to punish transgressions of the natural law. In civil society, social relationships are created and reproduced by the original compact and preserved by the legislative and executive powers that are surrendered to the polity. To Locke, the notion that there are important relationships only gifting can maintain is as remote to him as were the Americas in 1690.

This is evidenced by Locke's earlier and wholly mistaken interpretation of the "wild Indian's" relationship to the venison he takes, which is claimed to be ownership arising from his laboring on the common stock. But from the Native view, the deer is not a part of the common stock owned jointly by all humanity, and one does not make the venison property by laboring to take it from the common stock. Instead, not being owned by anyone—let alone the mass of humanity—the deer gives itself to the hunter, who is then obligated to perform as a counter-gift the appropriate acts of gratitude. This gifting exchange preserves and reproduces humanity's social relationships with other nonhuman persons.

While granting all of the merits of Mauss's account of indigenous gifting traditions, there are a few problems, one of which is exposed by Godelier—and which, interestingly enough, mirrors a mistake Locke makes. Locke's account of the origin of civil society focuses exclusively on barter between individuals, while Mauss considers only gifting between various groups (i.e., families, clans, or tribes). However, as Godelier (1999) points out, there are certainly *both* kinds of exchange in all societies.[10] What marks the difference between Native and Western traditions is the importance of each kind of exchange in the *internal* workings of societies (158). William Penn may have observed "a fine gun, coat, or other thing" pass twenty Shawnee hands before it stuck, because gifting is the primary mode of exchange *within* Shawnee society, but it is quite likely that the exchange that initially placed those European goods in Shawnee hands was a trade and not a gift.

Godelier makes an even more important observation that Mauss overstates his case that in indigenous gifting traditions *"everything*—food, women, children, property, talismans, land, labour services, priestly func-tions, and ranks—is there for passing on and for balancing accounts" (14; emphasis added). Although there are obligations to give, accept, and recipro-cate some material and nonmaterial objects and events to maintain balance and reinforce relationships in Native traditions, there are also things that are immune or exempt from gifting performances. Indeed, Godelier (1999) discovers an obligation *not* to part with some objects of a sacred nature; there are some objects that *must be kept* in order to maintain the kind of equilibrium in relationships necessary in indigenous societies[11] (108–210).

Perhaps the most problematic part of Mauss's account of gift exchange in Native societies is that, in the final analysis, it is every bit as consequen-tialist as the utilitarian moral theory he disdains. The utilitarian bases moral obligations on the nonmoral outcomes of actions—the maximization of good consequences for as many people as possible. But according to Mauss, the gifting member of a Native society is likewise motivated by consequences—*the largely negative consequences from not fulfilling the obligations to gift, accept or reciprocate!* One is obligated to gift to curry favor from ancestors, gain rank, win at potlatch or reinforce alliances—and if one doesn't, then something bad is bound to happen. Perhaps the gift's spirit will punish the offender, or the offender will lose rank or face. No doubt some Native stories *do* teach that bad consequences befall those who flout their gifting obligations; that is clearly the moral message conveyed by "Coyote, Iktome, and the Rock." However, Mauss fails to see or fully explore other sorts of moral grounds and motives for gifting, found especially in American Indian traditions, some of which—respect, generosity, and gratitude—are *not* consequentialist. And Mauss leaves largely undeveloped the *positive* consequentialist ground for the obligation to gift, namely, the obligation to balance accounts and maintain equilibrium for the overall good of persons—both human and non-human—in the American Indian nexus of relationships.

We observed in the last chapter that an American Indian kinship group is composed of spirit persons of various human and nonhuman out-ward forms—human and animal, plant and place, physical force and cardinal direction—all of whom are of equal value and stand in moral and social relationships with each other—relationships that are based upon *respect*, the fundamental Native moral value or attitude. As Lorraine Mayer (2007) stated it, respect—along with responsibility and relationship—are the three "Rs" characterizing the indigenous way of being in the world.[12] And, as I was taught by a tribal elder at a gathering many years back when he learned that I was studying philosophy, "The bedrock for the Shawnee is respect for other people and respect for all other living things" (Norton-Smith 2003:

26). So, one is obligated to give, accept, and reciprocate a gift in Native traditions as Mauss discovers, but neither solely nor principally because bad consequences will result from not doing so, although this must be a consideration, as we learn from Coyote's mistake. There are occasions on which one must give a gift out of respect for the recipient—and *nothing* could show more disrespect than to reject a gift; no wonder the Maori considered such a slight to be an act of war. Finally, to accept a gift is to receive a symbol of respect from another, and the gift obligates the recipient to show respect in return, to reciprocate.

Moreover, given that the spirit persons of various human and nonhuman forms in the American Indian kinship group are related to each other as *kin*—with all of the connections and affections, discords and disunities one finds in *family*—the obligation to gift is also grounded in the obligation *to care for* and *to be generous to* the members of an extended family, to one's kinfolk, as Martin eloquently expresses:

> [H]unters and gatherers acquired the powers of the bush, the desert, the plain, the tundra and sea, by sharing the qualities and powers of the creatures who, it was said, owned each distinctive sphere. These nonhuman people (spirit beings) were mentors and benefactors, giving counsel (through visions, dreams, trances, divinations, songs, and manner of life) and offering their flesh out of affection, even pity, for the "wingless, finless, gill-less, naked creatures" with such ingenious hands and clever voices. Thus say countless stories collected over the past five centuries. Underpinning the relationship with the spirits of the earth was a tenacious confidence that man and woman are taken care of by this commonwealth, through the principle of the *gift*: creatures gave themselves of their own free will. (1999: 8–9)

Of course, one cannot respectfully accept the gift of the flesh of an animal benefactor or a medicinal plant from a Grandfather, given to a kinsman out of affection, without *gratitude*, and so we have another nonconsequentialist ground for the Native obligation to reciprocate a gift. Laurie Whitt (2004) observes that traditional healers will address and offer thanks with tobacco to medicinal plants for gifting themselves to be used for healing (96). Indeed, the grateful offer of tobacco for the counsel from an elder or the lesson from a storyteller—or even for the favor of a letter written to the university registrar on behalf of a Native student—is a commonplace in Indian country.

Native people have been gifted much; they and the other peoples of the earth—plants and animals among them—live together in community in a place of unsurpassed beauty; indeed, a theme in Calvin Martin's *The Way of the Human Being* is that beauty infuses the indigenous world while the Western world is ruled by a ruthless taskmaster—time. The performance of world-renewing ceremonies at particular sacred sites on behalf and with the aid of other peoples of creation is an important way that this gift is reciprocated, and, as Deloria explains, these ceremonies are performed out of gratitude:

> [T]he ceremonies have very little to do with individual or tribal prosperity. Their underlying theme is one of gratitude expressed by human beings on behalf of all forms of life. They act to complete and renew the entire cosmos present in its specific realizations, so that in the last analysis one might describe ceremonials as the cosmos becoming thankfully aware of itself. (1999: 332)

Perhaps the most important moral ground for the obligations to gift, accept, and reciprocate, one that Mauss recognizes but does not fully develop, is the obligation to "balance accounts," to help promote and maintain equilibrium for the overall good of persons—both human and nonhuman—in the Native nexus of relationships. As Martin (1999) poetically observes, "In a world where everything breathes with life, has motion, is intelligent with thought, and is kinsman, equilibrium can work only when everything is exchanged as a *gift*, rather than through theft, stratagem, or 'main force' " (62).

In fact, a second important reason for the performance of world-renewing ceremonies—understood as gifts to other people in the world—is to restore and maintain equilibrium in the world, to renew connections to other nonhuman members of the Native community, and to recreate the world. Indeed, traditional tribal people have a *moral responsibility* to perform these ceremonies on behalf of other peoples in the world (Deloria 1999: 331).

But to understand just how the gift promotes and maintains equilibrium, we must return to Mauss's important observation that in the Native gifting performance a part of the giver is conveyed by and through the gift; the gift—even after the recipient accepts it—in part belongs to or remains a part of the giver. Moreover, the giver has influence over the gift given, how it is held, used or given away. Unlike its Western counterpart, wherein the giver has no further claim on or investment in the gift after it is accepted, the indigenous gift bears a part of giver that obliges its reciprocation, and in so doing creates and reinforces bonds and relationships between human and nonhuman persons in the Native world. As Whitt (2004) observes, "The giving of gifts establishes a relationship between those involved; their circulation within the human world, as well as between the human and nonhuman world, acknowledges and enhances the community" (197). So we see the empowering and transformative nature of the indigenous gifting performance with a symbol: The performance transforms the symbol, the gift—whether it is a material object or ritual ceremony—into an animate, ensouled thing with the power to unite and bind human and nonhuman familial members, to express generosity and gratitude, and to renew and recreate the world.

How, then, does gifting—understood as a performance with a symbol—categorize and order, recategorize and reorder the world? Returning to Godelier's observation that societies are characterized by the principal *internal* mode of exchange, that is, the most common sort of exchange of goods and services between members of the society, then gifting performances contribute to distinguishing members from nonmembers of the society, thus organizing the Native world. Additionally, Carli Waller made the observation that *not* gifting or *not* accepting can be as efficacious in categorizing the world; in gifting traditions like the Maori, she argues, neither gifting nor accepting organizes the world into states of war and antagonism, or states of peace and alliance. Finally, and most importantly, the Indian gifting performance in all of its manifestations—from the passing of a fine gun or coat from hand-to-hand, to the world-renewal ceremony performed at a sacred place—restores and maintains balance and equilibrium in the American Indian constructed world.

Closing Remarks About the Semantic Potency of Performances

We close by returning to the Black Elk narrative to observe yet another ceremony he performs in order to see how a Native performance with a symbol is potent, transformative, and helps construct an American Indian world. We are now familiar with the great vision Black Elk had as a child; we also know that "a man who has a vision is not able to use the power of it until after he has performed the vision on earth for the people to see" (2000: 157). Hence, it is necessary for Black Elk to perform the bison ceremony in order to understand and release its power.

With the help of Fox Belly, a wise old medicine man, and another tribal member, One Side, Black Elk begins by preparing a sacred place—full of symbols and symbolism—for the performance:

> First we made a sacred place like a bison wallow at the center
> of the nation's hoop, and there we set up a sacred tepee. Inside

this we made the circle of the four quarters. Across the circle
from south to north we painted a red road, and Fox Belly made
little bison tracks all along on both sides of it, meaning that
the people should walk there with the power and endurance of
the bison, facing the great white cleansing wind of the world.
Also, he placed at the north end of the road the cup of water,
which is the gift of the west, so that the people, while leaning
against the great wind with the endurance of bison, would be
going toward the water of life. (159)

Once the sacred place was set, Black Elk, painted red and clad in ceremonial
bison horns, a sacred herb and an eagle feather, performed the walk of the
red road with One Side while Fox Belly sang a sacred song:

> Revealing this, they walk.
> A sacred herb—revealing it, they walk.
> Revealing this, they walk.
> The sacred life of the bison—revealing it, they walk.
> Revealing this, they walk.
> A sacred eagle feather—revealing it, they walk.
> Revealing them, they walk.

The eagle and the bison—like relatives they walk. (159)
The two left the tepee at the conclusion of the ceremony, and the people
"flocked around"—especially the sick, who came to be cured by Black Elk's
newfound healing powers. The little children came as well, to drink from
the symbolic wooden cup of water "that their feet might know the good
red road that leads to health and happiness" (160).

Now, we embraced Goodman's constructivist view that linguistic
versions of the world—statements, theories, and models—make worlds by
identifying, categorizing, and ordering sense experiences. However, in American Indian traditions the performance of other sorts of unwritten symbols
becomes the principal vehicle of meaning and world-constructing process.
Symbols, like Black Elk's vision, the cup of water and eagle feather, the
painted red road and the healing herb, have significance, but they are largely
impotent until Black Elk performs with them in the ceremony; the water
now guides the future of the children and the sacred herb becomes medicine
to cure the sick. Moreover, Black Elk is *himself* transformed by performing
the vision for the people, for he comes to understand and release the power
of the bison to heal. Finally, the ceremony represents and reaffirms the
relationships between the people and the bison and the eagle—"like relatives they walk." The bison ceremony supports and strengthens the Native

categorization and ordering of experiences, thus contributing to the creation and recreation of an actual American Indian world.

An important part of Black Elk's bison ceremony is the preparation of a sacred place in the nation's *hoop* in which to perform the ceremony. Chapter 7 shows that the symbolic elements of the sacred space, such as the *circle* of the four quarters—south, west, north, and east—reflect a more thoroughgoing Native ontological frame of reference. This, the last of our common themes, is circularity as a world-ordering principle in American Indian world version.

7

Circularity as a
World-Ordering Principle

This chapter begins with the commonplace that American Indian religious traditions can be distinguished from Western religious traditions in that the former focus on space, place, and nature, whereas the latter are framed by time, events, and history. I then present a constructivist interpretation of Donald Fixico's reflection that American Indian philosophy is a circular philosophy. Specifically, I propose that Western and Native world versions are distinguished by fundamentally different world-ordering principles: Western versions are framed by a linear ordering principle, whereas Indian versions assume a circular ordering principle. I conclude that these fundamentally different ways of ordering experiences accounts for the Western preoccupation with time and the Native focus on space.

Goodman Briefly Revisited

It was almost one year ago that I first began thinking about my bird feeder in the backyard. It's now early April, the daffodils are just beginning to come up and the robins have been back about a month. As a prelude to our discussion of the fourth and last common theme in American Indian world versions—circularity as a world-ordering principle—it might be useful to remind ourselves of some of the fundamentals of Goodman's constructivism that we considered so long ago on that beautiful day in May.

Remember that the pure content of our sense experiences alone underdetermines reality, that any one of a number of radically different actual worlds is consistent with experience. Facts are fabricated and worlds are created by the devices of language; but as we saw in Chapter 6, sense experiences can be categorized and organized by other sorts of performances with symbols—prayer, dance, ceremony, and gifting among them. Composition, decomposition, and weighting are among the world-organizing processes that we've considered, and *ordering*—creating various patterns in sense experience—is a particularly important world-constructing process. By now, it is a commonplace that "we are all relatives" is one world-ordering principle Indians employ, that is, one way to relate and organize experiences. This chapter explores how Natives use *circularity* as a world-ordering principle, as a way to pattern spatial and temporal experiences. Fixico (2003) says that "circles and cycles are central to the world" (1). *We say that creating circular patterns in sense experience is central to the making of the American Indian world.*

Finally, recall that we embraced Goodman's view that true world versions construct *actual* worlds, and that the ultimate acceptability of a world version is sufficient for its truth. However, we argued that Goodman's criteria for the ultimate acceptability of a world version—deductive validity and inductive rightness, utility and simplicity—are culturally biased against non-Western world versions. So, we proposed that the criteria for the ultimate acceptability of a world version be reinterpreted with respect to a *cultural frame of reference*, determined by asking, "For whom is the world version ultimately acceptable?" Once we have in hand culturally sophisticated criteria for the rightness of a world version, we can judge whether or not a proposed version satisfies those criteria, hence constructs an actual world.

Time, Events, and History or Space, Place, and Nature?

One of the most common characterizations of the difference between Western and American Indian world versions is that the Western view is framed in some fundamental way by a conception of *time*, whereas Native world versions are likewise fundamentally framed by a conception of *space*. Deloria (1994), perhaps the most prominent Native advocate of and apologist for the distinction, draws several conclusions about each tradition from this dichotomy. It is first of all a source of confusion because the two traditions are *incommensurable*; Indians consider their places to be of greatest significance, whereas Westerners find meaning in the progression of events over time, so there are fundamental differences in meaning between the two world versions—differences that must be recognized, by the way, before each tradition understands the other:

> American Indians hold their lands—places—as having the highest possible meaning, and all their statements are made with this reference point in mind. [Western European] Immigrants review the movement of their ancestors across the continent as a steady progression of basically good events and experiences,

thereby placing history—time—in the best possible light. When one group is concerned with the philosophical problem of space and the other with the philosophical problem of time, then the statements of either group do not make much sense when transferred from one context to the other without the proper consideration of what is taking place. (62–63)

Deloria (1999) then draws some consequences about religion from the dichotomy between the Western preoccupation with the temporal and the Native focus on the spatial. "Christianity," he says, "has always placed a major emphasis on the idea of history" (295). As a result, he maintains, Christianity assumes that the most significant human religious entities are *events* organized linearly in time. Knowing the places where Jesus was born or crucified is largely irrelevant to Christian doctrine—but there simply would be no Christian religion without the event of the resurrection. Moreover, from the fulfillment of past prophecies to the anticipated end days forecast by "Revelations," the movement of Christianity is temporal (295). On the other hand, Deloria (1994) continues, the historical memory of religious events is of very little importance in Native religious traditions. Instead,

> The structure of their religious traditions is taken directly from the world around them, from their relationships with other forms of life. Context is therefore all-important for both practice and the understanding of reality. The places where revelations were experienced were remembered and set aside as locations where, through rituals and ceremonials, the people could *once again* communicate with the spirits. . . . It was not what people believed to be true that was important but what they experienced as true. (66–67; emphasis added)

As a consequence, Deloria observes, almost all tribal religions have a sacred place or geographic feature at its center—a mountain, plateau, or river among them. This religious center—this sacred place—helps the people to locate themselves with respect to their lands, the cardinal directions, and their other nonhuman relations. Despite removals and the other misfortunes that have befallen the tribes, Deloria (1994) concludes, sacred places are "permanent fixtures" in their religious life and understanding (67). And so we have a *second* dichotomy arising from the Western concern with time and the Native focus on space, namely, the importance of the *sacred event* in Western religions as opposed to the *sacred place* in Indian religious traditions.[1]

There is yet a third way the distinction between time and space manifests itself, namely, in the Western tradition's alienation from, and the

Native embrace of, the natural world. This is an important theme in Calli-cott (1989: 177–201) as well as Martin (1999), who contrasts the distinction between the two traditions—and our place in those traditions—as being in time and history and being of the earth and in beauty, with our true humanity—our "proper story"—of a piece with the latter:

> Not as swimmers struggling to stay afloat in the dark river of time but as vessels of beauty: let us so imagine ourselves. Beauty has an older claim on us than does time; beauty was there in the beginning before time was conceived; it was inherent in the originating Word, the idea and its pronouncement. Time is but beauty's scaffolding. (15–16)

And so we have a pretty sharp distinction between *time*, *events*, and *history* in the Western tradition, and *space*, *place*, and *nature* in the American Indian tradition. But although this difference is undeniable, I suggest that the dichotomy between the Western preoccupation with *time*, *events*, and *history*, and the Native focus on *space*, *place*, and *nature* is based on an even more fundamental distinction.

Circularity as a World-Ordering Principle

We have made the constructivist point before, but it bears repeating: Pat-terns in sense experience are where you find them. We *create* patterns in experience rather than *discover* them—as anyone familiar with constellations in the night sky knows. Consider, for example, the stars in a fictional sky in Figure 7.1. There are a number of ways we might organize the stars into "constellations." If we employed a linear ordering principle, then one way our fictional night sky might be patterned appears in Figure 7.2. However, if we employed a circular ordering principle, then our fictional night sky might have the "constellation" appearing in Figure 7.3.

The point of the illustration is that there are various ways we can and do organize *spatial* experiences—various patterns we can and do create. But there are, as well, different ways we can order *temporal* experiences. Consider, for example, the formal logic final examinations I have administered every semester since 1988. These events can be ordered linearly in time, so that each exam occupies a point on a directed temporal continuum, either before or after other exams in time. However, if we employ a circular temporal ordering principle, then a final examination is the recurring culminating event in an ongoing cycle of courses. In this respect, logic finals occur as regularly as the seasons—another circular temporal ordering. As with

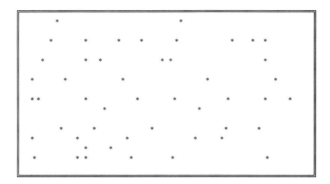

Figure 7.1. The fictional night sky

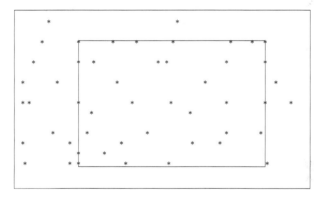

Figure 7.2. The sky ordered linearly

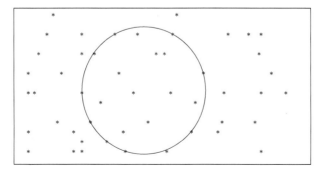

Figure 7.3. The sky ordered circularly

spatial experiences, then, there are various ways we can impose an order on temporal experiences.

Now, we have seen that the Western tradition holds *events in time* as the most significant, whereas American Indians regard *places in space* as the most meaningful. I propose, however, that there are equally significant conceptions of both time and space—and both event and place—in each tradition. What is importantly different, however, is the most "natural" ordering principle each tradition uses to pattern both temporal and spatial experiences: The Western tradition is fond of a linear ordering principle, whereas Natives employ a circular ordering principle. This is not to say, of course, that these ordering principles are unique to each tradition; indeed, I moved quite freely between linear and circular orderings in my two previous illustrations. However, I maintain that the most "natural" way to order in Native and Western traditions is circularly and linearly, respectively. As Fixico (2003) observes with respect to the former, "In order to understand Indian people and their ways of life, it is evident that the 'circle' occupies an integral role in the beliefs of American Indians. Patterns and daily norms of American Indian groups involve the circle as a part of their many cultures" (42).

Let us first notice how a linear ordering principle manifests itself in the practices and preconceptions of the Western world version. We see it in the assumption that societies progress over time in a linear fashion from the primitive to the civilized, as expressed so ably by Powell (1877) and other cultural anthropologists until fairly recently. A similar assumption is expressed about the linear progress of science and technology, as each scientific model or theory is closer to the truth than the one it supersedes, and each new technological innovation constitutes an "advance." The Christian can be responsible for "original sin" only if there is a linear, unbroken chain of responsibility extending back to Adam's initial indiscretion,[2] and philosophical determinism makes sense only if there is an unbroken causal chain of events from some original physical event. Logical reasoning is a linear progression of valid inferences from premises to conclusion, and circularity—although valid—is rejected as if it were fallacy. Distance and temperature are conceived of linearly—although they need not be—and are so measured. The geometry of our dwellings—the straight lines and right angles—embodies the linear ordering of the spatial. And Fixico (2003) insightfully and rightfully observes that the very goal-oriented structure of Western life—and its consequences—is the product of "a linear mind":

> The linear person, who is goal oriented, is a part of the mainstream of looking ahead, keeping one's head down and working hard, or not looking back for someone might be gaining on you. In such

a view of only looking ahead, a person does not see what or who is either side of him or her. Perhaps this is why so many people experience stress in the modern American society. (174)

In American Indian traditions, however, circularity orders both temporal and spatial sense experiences, and so virtually all other facets of Native life, especially religion. Indeed, it is sometimes hard to distinguish the temporal from the spatial in an Indian circular ordering of experiences; but this shouldn't be too surprising, for we have now long known that the drawing of sharp distinctions is a Western predilection, but not a Native one. Notice, for example, that it is universally acknowledged that indigenous peoples are very close observers of the natural world and all of the cycles in its workings—seasonal cycles, lunar phases, animal migrations, and the growth of various plants. Indeed, hunter–gatherer societies *had* to observe, create, and operate in accordance with seasonal patterns, with cyclical patterns imposed on *temporal* experiences—the ripening of berries in spring, late summer corn harvests, autumn migrations, and winter hunts—in order to survive. But such seasonal circular orderings are also *spatial* orderings—harvests and hunts are events in both time *and* space. As a result, American Indian traditions came to regard cycles and circles as the primary temporal *and* spatial ordering principle, to develop "tribal philosophies based on the circle," as Fixico (2003) puts it (49). With respect to the circular patterning of the temporal, he conveys that

[b]y studying the changes of the seasons and observing the lives of animals and plants as a part of nature, native logic became grounded in the central idea of a continuum of events that seemed familiar. Nature repeated itself in a continuous series of cycles and seasons of circular patterns. Animals and humans live the same various stages of life starting with birth, infancy, puberty, adulthood, old age, then death, and life repeated the same phases with the next generation. (49–50)

However, the circular ordering of the spatial is just as prevalent and important in Native traditions—and is, again, closely tied to and integrated with the temporal. Indeed, Fixico explains that the Muscogee Creek "Circle of Life," which includes all things consisting of spiritual energy in their natural, cyclical, seasonal—that is, *temporal*—comings and goings, "begins with the cardinal directions"—a *spatial* ordering (42–46). The Muscogee Creeks are neither alone nor unique in this view, for it is widely held by American Indian peoples that the powers of the cardinal directions are associated with the powers of the seasons or parts of the day—*temporal* orderings. We have seen before Black Elk's (2000) interpretation of the sacred pipe of the Lakota:

> These four ribbons hanging here on the stem are the four quar-
> ters of the universe. The black one is for the west where the
> thunder beings live to send us rain; the white one for the north,
> whence comes the great white cleaning wind; the red one for
> the east, whence springs the light and where the morning star
> lives to give men wisdom; the yellow for the south, whence
> come the summer and the power to grow. (2)

So, to the Lakota traditionalist the power of the west sends rain, and the north brings the winter wind; the power of the east is where the morning star lives, and the south sends the summer. Each of the spatial directions, then, is also associated with a cyclical seasonal (i.e., temporal) event or occurrence.

Dark Rain Thom (1994) shares that the Shawnee spatial cardinal directions are likewise associated with the temporal cycles, either daily or seasonal. The Grandfather of the east is associated with morning and "tends to advice for us to follow," and the Grandfather of the west listens to eve- ning prayers; the Grandfather of the north rules half of the daylight and protects us over winter, and the Grandfather of the south rules the other half of the daylight and protects us over the summer (222–23). Again, we see in this Algonquin tradition that the spatial and temporal cycles are interconnected.

We find the same Native integration of spatial and temporal cycles in the work of Ted Jojola, who develops a model of an American Indian community identity he calls the *transformative model*, based on Pueblo clan migrations as recorded by petroglyph spirals found across the Southwest. These spirals have directionality; outward spirals indicate a circular clan migration from a home territory—a "centerplace"—outward in a journey "to gain experiential knowledge," whereas inward spirals chronicle the cir- cular homeward migration. Jojola (2004) argues that outward migrations were *transformative*; journeying to the edges of the world-transformed Pueblo clans—as journeys to the unknown often do—and migrations contributed to their collective knowledge and to their survival. Importantly, he considers one particular migration spiral that documents both spatial and temporal elements of the journey, incorporating symbols representing *both* the circular spatial path of clan migration and temporal cycles in the solstice calendar. But this shouldn't be surprising, given our position that there is no sharp distinction between circular spatial and temporal orderings in American Indian traditions.

Circularity as a principle that orders temporal and spatial experiences shapes and patterns all other facets of American Indian life, especially social life and practice—well beyond the more obvious circular orientation of Native camps, towns, and stomp grounds (Fixico 2003: 43). The cycle of the seasons determined most important tribal activities—foraging or planting, harvests or hunts—and in so doing assigned seasonal responsibilities to various tribal members; women are responsible for cultivation and it falls to men to hunt. As well, ceremonies and rituals, like the Shawnee spring and fall Bread Dances, are occasioned by the seasons. Gifting practices, wherein one is obligated to give, receive, and reciprocate a gift—and a performance which itself orders the American Indian world version—also embodies the circular pattern.

Perhaps most important, the principle of circularity orders the verification and transmission of knowledge; indeed, Fixico maintains that "[t]he concept of the circle is fundamental to understanding [Native] knowledge" (45). Circularity can be seen in the verification of knowledge, for we have seen that tribal tradition is one way to verify that an action, procedure or performance is respectfully successful in achieving a goal. We can easily imagine a tribal elder explaining that, "this way has always worked, so we'll do it that way now, and so will you pass it down to your children." And the transmission of knowledge is, as well, circular in form, as Fixico's *own* presentation of an American Indian circular philosophy demonstrates—a style of presentation that may be mistaken for mere *repetition*:

> One might say that the Indian mind is *abstract*, and confused with repetition. But another person might say that numerous examples stress the same point as stories told with the same message in mind for teaching the listener. Even *these* written words may seem repetitious, but in the circular way the purpose is met to prevent misunderstanding. It is a teaching tool.[3] (56; emphasis added)

So, we have seen that circularity orders both the temporal and the spatial, and so all other facets of American Indian life—communal and social, epistemic and religious. Indeed, Black Elk (2000) envisions the place, the health, the future—and indeed, the spirits—of the Lakota people and all their relatives *spatially* and *circularly*—as sacred hoops. In his great vision he conveys the following:

> I was standing on the highest mountain of them all, and round about beneath me was the whole hoop of the world. And while I stood there I saw more than I can tell and I understood more

than I saw; for I was seeing in a sacred manner the shapes as
they must live together like one being. And I saw that the sacred
hoop of my people was one of many hoops that made one circle,
wide as daylight and as starlight, and in the center grew one
mighty flowering tree to shelter all the children of one mother
and one father. And I saw that it was holy. (33)

But an interesting question still remains to be considered: How does the
proposal that circularity orders the Native world version account for or
relate to the view that the *sanctity of place*—framed by a conception of
space—distinguishes the American Indian tradition from the Western tradition, which is framed by a conception of time? That is the question to
which we now turn.

Circularity and Sacred Places

We begin by reviewing Deloria's categorization and description of four kinds
of sacred places. Members of the first kind of sacred place are sites sanctified
by *human* activities or events, such as the Gettysburg battlefield or the site of
the attack on the World Trade Center. As Deloria (1999) observes, these are
usually sites of violence—"exquisitely dear to us"—but they are not places
where humans have experienced anything "mysteriously religious," places
where "Indians would say something holy has appeared in an otherwise
secular situation" (329). This is characteristic of a second kind of sacred
place, exemplified by Buffalo Gap in the Black Hills of South Dakota and
by the Petroglyph National Monument in New Mexico.

Deloria then describes places that are regarded as sites of "overwhelm-
ing holiness," where powerful nonhuman spirit persons make themselves
known to human persons, exemplified in the Western tradition by the many
European Christian churches built on the same sites earlier occupied by
pagan temples. Most such Native sites in this third kind of sacred place are
not widely known outside of Indian circles, but some—like Bear Butte—are
well known (331). Finally, given that the world is unfixed and unfinished—
always being created and recreated through the actions and performances
of human and nonhuman persons of all sorts—it is possible that places
not now sanctified by human or nonhuman activity or intervention may
become sites of future revelation. "Consequently," Deloria concludes about
this fourth kind of sacred place, "we always look forward to the revelation
of new sacred places and ceremonies" (333).

Important to our discussion of the relationship between Native sacred places and circularity as an American Indian world-ordering principle is the moral obligation Natives have to perform specific rituals and ceremonies at specific sacred sites periodically at specific times. We have already visited the Shawnee spring and fall Bread Dances—which are at the heart of the yearly ritual cycle—and which are held out of gratitude to the Creator for agricultural and hunting bounty, and to reaffirm the complementary roles of woman as cultivator and man as hunter. Other sorts of ceremonies periodically performed at specific sacred sites are renewal ceremonies, re-establishing equilibrium between and promoting the prosperity of all persons, human and nonhuman alike:

> People have been commanded to perform ceremonies at these holy places so that the earth and all its forms of life might survive and prosper. Evidence of this moral responsibility that sacred places command has come through the testimony of traditional people when they have tried to explain . . . that they must perform certain ceremonies at specific times and places in order that the sun may continue to shine, the earth prosper, and the stars remain in the heavens. (Deloria 1999: 331)

Now, I argue that because these various Native ceremonial cycles are both spatially and temporally regular—performed at the same sites at the same seasonal times—we should perhaps revisit the view that American Indian religious traditions are largely framed by the spatial and not the temporal. Instead, I propose that Natives employ a circular world-ordering principle to order *both* spatial and temporal experiences. Moreover, I suspect that traditional Indians do not sharply distinguish the temporal from the spatial in the circular ordering of experiences. Hunts and harvests have both spatial and temporal dimensions, and so, too, do religious ceremonies and rituals performed at specific times and places. This means that unlike the Western understanding wherein *place* has only a spatial dimension, Native sacred places have both *spatial* and *temporal* dimensions—and those dimensions, as Fixico teaches, are "based on the circle" (49). And there is no better illustration of the integration of the Native circular ordering of the spatial and the temporal—and none closer to my heart—than the Hopewell sacred places located throughout what is now central and southern Ohio.[4]

The Hopewell Middle Woodland culture is believed to have flourished from around 100 B.C.E. to about 500 C.E. They were hunters, gatherers, and early agriculturalists who apparently had wide-ranging economic contacts with tribes across the continent, crafting religious and secular artifacts from precious metals like copper and silver, rare stones and minerals like mica and obsidian, as well as alligator and shark teeth (Romain 2000: 2). Their "artistic" skills were extraordinary, and their artifacts are breathtaking: Cowan (1996) presents some artifacts—intricate pipestone effigies, falcon-shaped boat stones, and copper breastplates among them—and then considers some of their social implications.

Like the earlier Adena and the later Fort Ancient Indians, the Hopewell were "mound builders," constructing massive geometrically shaped earthworks, burial mounds and cremation pits, terraces, platforms, and walled passages that served as their sacred ceremonial sites. Romain speculates that Hopewell ritual ceremonies—determined by significant solar and lunar events—concerned "passage from this world to the next, death and rebirth, world renewal, and creation" (8). Byers (1996) concurs. A few Hopewell sites like Fort Ancient in Warren County still serve as ceremonial grounds for contemporary American Indians.

It should not be surprising that most Hopewell earthworks have been destroyed or defiled by decades of modern agriculture, development, and artifact hunters; indeed, the complex I want to consider, the Newark Earthworks in Licking County, Ohio, was deeded by court order to the Ohio Historical Society in 1933, but it is still defiled by the Moundbuilders Country Club—a private golf course created in 1910 (Moundbuilders).

The Newark Earthworks were mapped in 1848 by Ephraim Squier and Edwin Davis (1998). Only two major features of the original extensive site survive, the Fairground Circle and the Octagon-Observatory Circle, both of which are contained within quadrilaterals on the Squier and Davis map. These are massive sacred sites; the Fairground Circle is 1,190 feet in diameter, whereas the Observatory Circle is 1,054 feet in diameter and its connecting Octagon has an approximate area of 40 acres; indeed, the Octagon-Observatory Circle *encloses* the 18-hole Moundbuilders golf course (Romain 2000).

Although a popular nineteenth-century speculation was that at least some of the more irregularly shaped Hopewell earthworks served a defensive function, a significant study of the Newark Earthworks by Hively and Horn (1982) suggests that there are seventeen lunar alignments incorporated into the works, with a number of alignments to the major and minor lunar "standstills"—the major rising and setting points in the 18.6-year lunar cycle—associated with the complex. Romain (2000) concurs with Hively and Horn that the longitudinal axis of the Octagon-Observatory Circle (see the Squier and Davis map in Figure 7.4) aligns with the moon's maximum north rise, and the entrance to the Fairground Circle (see the Squier and Davis map in Figure 7.4) aligns with the moon's minimum north rise. Hively and Horn (2006) documents a statistical analysis of five lunar

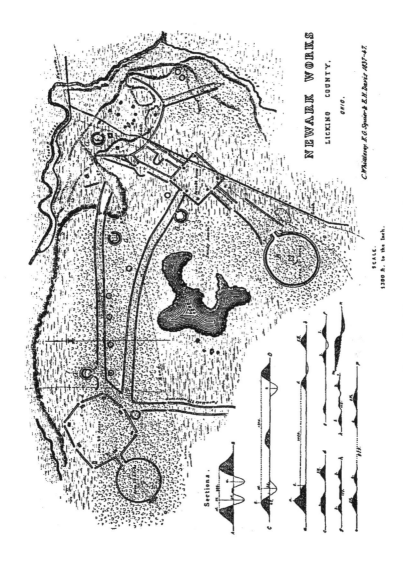

Figure 7.4. The Newark Earthworks

alignments associated with the Octagon, concluding that it is unlikely that they were constructed either accidentally or out of simple curiosity about lunar motions. In short, there is compelling evidence that the Newark site is a Hopewell sacred place that is also the physical embodiment of a lunar cycle.

Now, I argue that the Newark complex is a sacred site that exemplifies both circular spatial and temporal dimensions of Hopewell ceremonial life, that Hopewell ceremonies were performed at the same sacred places—demonstrating a spatial circularity—and at regular sacred times—demonstrating a temporal circularity. So, their ceremonial life, hence all aspects of life, were determined by a circular ordering principle. First, the Newark sacred site exemplifies a spatial circularity far beyond the obvious shape of the pair of nearly perfect earthwork circles. For Byers (1996) and Romain (2000, 2005) argue that the geometrical shapes of the earthworks have cosmological significance, symbolizing various aspects of Hopewell sacred cosmology, and the circle plays a prominent role in that world version. Indeed, Romain (2000) speculates—perhaps incautiously—that Hopewell circular earthworks symbolized or represented the earth. Although I agree with Lepper (1996) that the true symbolism of Hopewellian geometry may be beyond our ken, it is not far-fetched to believe that the shape of the Newark earthwork has a religious or ceremonial significance—and spatial circularity is conspicuous.

However, this alone will not make the point that the Hopewell used a spatial ordering principle because their earthworks are sometimes also shaped in squares and octagons. Instead, I propose that as a sacred place to which the Hopewell returned again and again at appointed times—times incorporated into the very structure of the site—there is evidence of a circularity akin to the *spatial* dimensions of harvests and hunts, gatherings and foragings—seasonal activities that have both spatial and temporal dimensions.

That a circular temporal ordering principle frames the Newark complex is obvious, given the evidence that the earthworks are gigantic embodiments of an 18.6-year lunar cycle. Indeed, Romain (2000) provides compelling evidence—compelling to a philosopher, anyway—that other Hopewell sites across central and southern Ohio are aligned to various other cyclical solar and lunar events—for example, Mound City in Ross County is aligned to the summer solstice, whereas the Quadranaou Mound at the Marietta Earthworks in Washington County is aligned to the winter solstice.

I conclude, then, that the Hopewell employed a circular ordering principle in framing both the spatial and temporal dimensions of their sacred places, hence ordering their ceremonies, rituals, and all other aspects of life. So, scholars like Deloria (1999) are justified in holding the view that the sanctity of place—*framed in part by a circular spatial ordering principle*—distinguishes the Native tradition from the Western tradition—*which is framed in part by a linear temporal ordering principle*. And scholars like Fixico (2003) are justified in holding the view that the American Indian religious tradition—indeed, all aspects of Native life—is framed by the circle and the cycle—*by both circular spatial and temporal ordering principles*.

Closing Remarks About Circularity as a World-Ordering Principle

Fixico (2003) closes his thoughtful reflections on an American Indian circular philosophy by stressing the symbolism and significance of the center of the circle—or the *sphere*, if we "remind ourselves to look up and down as well"—to the Muscogee Creek, Crow, and Navajo traditions specifically, but then to Native folks in general. For the traditional Muscogee Creek the center of the sphere is the seventh direction, "well-being and the balance of life"; for the Crow, the center is one's connection to the Creator; and for the Dine—who view all things in life to be interconnected—one sees in all directions in that stage of life that is the full circle and its center. In general, Native people regard all natural processes and places—including a human life—as circular, and that "things come full circle" toward the end of life. But the center of the circle of one's life is the place of peace, balance and equilibrium (173–76).

As constructivists, we have long observed that there are many ways that our experiences may be ordered, for "patterns are where you find them." The Western mind employs a deeply ingrained linear ordering principle, which undergirds a linear conception of time and space; indeed, Kant even proposed that linear time and Euclidean space were *a priori* intuitions. However, the American Indian mind uses a circular ordering principle—as deeply ingrained as its Western counterpart—which frames the Native conceptions of time and space; circular patterns are found in both temporal and spatial experiences. This means that American Indian sacred places, where Native people are obligated to return again and again at specific times to perform ceremonies of gratitude and renewal for the good of human and nonhuman persons alike, are imbued with both temporal and spatial circularities—and significance.

8

The Dance of Person and Place

This final chapter focuses on the interpretation of our four common themes in American Indian philosophy, relatedness and circularity as world-ordering principles, the expansive conception of persons, and the semantic potency of performance, as *a dance of person and place*. It also presents some closing reflections, speculations, and consequences of this constructivist rendering of the Native world.

American Indian Philosophy as a Dance of Person and Place

In keeping with the American Indian common theme of *circularity as a world-ordering principle*, we return to our beginning, to my backyard one year ago on that beautiful day in mid-May. Now it's the *same* time of year, the *same* place, and the *same* bird feeder—and it is *still* not moving, by the way—although the squirrels chewed it over the winter, so it's in need of repair. But, of course, the sameness of time, place, and feeder are fabricated facts, a part of my linguistically imposed ontological conception of the world.

It has been a pretty memorable year. I was honored to dance in the Shawnee spring Bread Dance for the first time, and I also had the honor of participating in a ceremony reconciling the differences between the Shawnee and the descendants of Col. William Crawford, who was brutally executed in 1782 in retaliation for the murder of ninety-six Christian Delaware Indians at Gnadenhutten. And, of course, we've had this time together, which has been empowering and transformative—rather like performances with symbols in American Indian traditions. Allow me to remind you of some of our investigations and findings.

After rehearsing important tenets of Nelson Goodman's constructive nominalism, the view that there is a plurality of internally consistent, equally privileged, well-made *actual* worlds constructed by true or right world versions, and that there are no objects or kinds of things independent of some world version or other, I argued that only a constructive *realism*—wherein world-constructing processes like composition and decomposition, collecting and sorting, and weighting and ordering are construed as kinds of human activities independent of and logically prior to any and all world versions—can rescue his constructivism from a self-referential paradox. Because Goodman's view is expressed in language, and because the only objects and kinds that exist are the ones created by symbol systems like language, it follows that the kinds of world-constructing processes to which he refers are relevant only within the bounds of his own constructive nominalism—a contemporary Western view in analytic philosophy; Goodman cannot give an account of the ways of world-making that extends beyond the limits of his own linguistically constructed world version.

Moreover, I argued that Goodman's criteria for the ultimate acceptability of a world version—where ultimate acceptability is sufficient for the truth of a version—are culturally biased against any non-Western world version, including an American Indian version. However, a constructivism that reinterprets the criteria for the rightness of a world version—including deductive validity, and inductive rightness and utility—in a culturally sophisticated way by posing the question "For whom is the world version ultimately acceptable?" will find a Native world version among those that construct internally consistent, well-made *actual* worlds. So, if words and other sorts of performances can make a plurality of radically different actual worlds—as maintained throughout this volume—and if the criteria for the ultimate acceptability of a world version are not restricted to a narrowly construed Western scientific rendering, then an ultimately acceptable American Indian world version—a true world version—constructs a radically different actual world, made, both literally and figuratively, by *the dance of person and place*.

Human persons dancing at particular places and times—determined by circles and cycles—*literally* make and remake the American Indian world, as when the Shawnee dance the Bread Dance. In a world that is neither mechanistic nor material, neither fixed nor finished, but is, rather, animate and aware, dynamic and unfolding, where creativity is the moving force and where "all things are related," persons participating in their required dances at the specified times and places return balance to and gratefully reaffirm their place—and the places of all other human and nonhuman persons—in that world.

More importantly, the *dance of person and place* serves as a *metaphor* for the way an American Indian world is made. We have seen that *dance* and all sorts of procedures, practices, and performances can identify, categorize, and order sense experiences; we have called this the *semantic potency of performance*. Besides dance, we have considered speech acts like prayers, songs, and storytellings, rituals such as renewal or naming ceremonies, and gifting. We have observed that performing with a symbol empowers the symbol and transforms the participants and the world—the story told has a spirit, the name performed cares for its bearer, the gift and its reciprocation maintains balance, and the dance expresses gratitude and renews the world. We have also seen that truth is a property of respectfully successful procedures, practices, and performances, verification is to be understood as the direct experience of the respectful success of a procedure, practice, or performance, and, finally, that the principal conception of knowledge in Native traditions is procedural knowledge. The world is not inert, fixed, and finished, but is being constantly created by the procedures and performances—in the broadest sense of the term, the *dances*—of *persons*.

Persons are animate "spirit beings" standing in a nexus of relationships—relationships grounded in and sustained by *respect*—with all sorts of human and nonhuman persons, including powerful spirit persons embodied as places, physical forces and cardinal directions, ancestors, nonhuman animals and plants—even the Earth itself. We have called this *the expansive conception of persons*. In a world teeming with persons, all of whom have their own needs and desires, emotions and volition, and good and bad impulses—some of whom are very powerful entities—we must be constantly mindful of our actions and their consequences. The wider Indian community, which includes persons of all types and stripes, is maintained and reinforced by the *circular* and *cyclical* obligations to offer, accept, and reciprocate gifts in order to reaffirm familial connections and to "balance accounts."

We agreed with the common observation that sacred places are central to Native religious traditions, and that this evidences a dichotomy between Indian space, place, and nature and Western time, event, and history. However, American Indians not only have a well-developed notion of time, but also of sacred events—like our earlier considered performances of specific dances at specific places. This suggests that there is another distinction between the two traditions, namely, a difference in the most natural ordering principles each uses to order experiences, with Native traditions using a *circular ordering principle*. Thus, like other seasonal events with both spatial and temporal dimensions, ceremonies—such as the dances of persons—at sacred places exhibit and embody both circular spatial and temporal properties and orderings.

Finally, and perhaps the most important for understanding the American Indian worldview, is *relatedness as a world-ordering principle*—"we are all related." Relatedness connects all human and nonhuman spirit persons in the American Indian community, and the conviction that everything is related motivates Natives to actively seek out connections from apparently disparate or unrelated experiences—that's why dances by persons at sacred places influence the world. There are no real distinctions between various branches of human knowledge—science and religion, philosophy and song—because everything is related, and, importantly, there are connections and interconnections, dependencies and interdependencies between *dances* and *persons* and *places* because "we are all related."

Consequences, Speculations, and Closing Reflections

An obvious consequence of the constructivist view I have advanced herein—one that will undoubtedly make *everyone* angry—is that the Western and American Indian world versions make equally *legitimate, actual* worlds. Scholars trained in the Western tradition—philosophers, anthropologists, and scientists among them—who hold the realist view that the workings of a mind-independent physical world are uniquely captured by the theories and models of Western science, and who also maintain that the American Indian worldview is merely a primitive antecedent to modern Western civilization, will look derisively upon my notion that the Native world is every bit as *actual* as its Western counterpart. On the other hand, Indians, who are as committed to the mind-independent existence of their world as Western realists, will justifiably object to the claim that a world version responsible for the untold and immeasurable decimation and destruction of the American Indian world—a decimation and destruction of Native dances, persons, and places—is *legitimate*. But those are inescapable consequences of the view I advance and I reluctantly embrace them. It will probably not assuage my offended friends from both traditions that I have tried to make only ontological and epistemological claims—*not moral claims*. However, my Native friends will correctly remind me that there is no real distinction between the epistemological, ontological, and moral. So be it.

Speaking of *moral claims*, another consequence about which I am more uncomfortable is that constructivist views seem to welcome *ethical relativism*, the moral view that there are no universal, absolute, or objective moral principles, statements, values, or judgments. This is to be distinguished from *cultural relativism*, the anthropological view that different cultures have different moral standards, for cultural relativism can be verified empirically, but ethical relativism cannot. The problem is that a radical relativism like Goodman's constructive nominalism cannot escape ethical relativism, but *ethical relativism is inconsistent*—hence, we have yet another challenge to his constructivism. Ethical relativism is inconsistent, because the statement of the view is itself the kind of universal statement whose existence it denies. If one counters that it is not to be understood as a universal *moral* statement, but is, rather, a *nonmoral* empirical generalization, then it is a statement of cultural relativism—*and we agree with that!*

So, if the kind of constructive realism I embrace, which maintains that there are kinds of human actions and activities independent of, and logically prior to, all world versions, cannot ground some sort of ethical realism, then it will be challenged in the same way as Goodman's constructive nominalism. I speculate, however, that there will be a way to ground such an ethical realism, given that there are "world version-independent" kinds of human actions, but there is not time now to develop the case; I've got to fix my bird feeder.

Finally, I close with a reflection and an apology. Although I am sure that any book poses special challenges, this one—with *The Burden* as its working title—has been particularly difficult to write. For, we've seen that any action, procedure or performance is normative, so I've been forced to ask myself daily not only the Western scholar's question—"Can I say this?"—but also the Shawnee question—"Should I say this?" Moreover, I know that some in the Native community disdain the very kind of work I have produced, as Lenore Keeshig-Tobias (2006) reflects in "Those Anthropologists," wherein she observes that anthropologists, sociologists, and historians "poke at our bones, our social systems and past events [to] try to tell us who we are." And when their books are ignored, "they feel sorry for us and write more books for themselves" (42). Some will now—perhaps justifiably—want to add *philosophers* to the list of anthropologists, sociologists, and historians who write books for themselves, books that apparently have little relevance for Indians. For those folks—some I know, respect, and revere—I offer a sincere apology.

pesalo no'ki tanakia!

Thomas

Notes

1. Common Themes in American Indian Philosophy

1. "kiwaakomelepwa" is a unique and compelling greeting. The stem or root "waakw-" has the sense of "knowing" or "having knowledge of" (Voegelin 1940: 416). The verb construction is the local animate "ki-ROOT-ele-pwa," which has the sense of "you (all)-VERB-(to) me." So the greeting is, literally, "You all are known to me." The letter "θ" stands for the phoneme "th" as in "theater."

2. My use of Nelson Goodman constructivism to explore American Indian Philosophy is not unique; indeed, Jim Cheney beautifully developed the notion of a "ceremonial world" in the spirit of a Goodmanian "reconception" of philosophy, wherein the concepts of *truth*, *certainty*, and *knowledge* are replaced by *rightness*, *adoption*, and *understanding*. Moreover, much that I have to say in my exploration supports—and is supported by—Professor Cheney's account of Native ethical-epistemology. "So much the better," observed Lee Hester in correspondence. "Though Jim's work . . . makes a different use of Goodman, it is also clear that his general points are consonant with yours. . . . The more we agree, the more we are likely to be on the right track."

Although Professor Cheney's development is breathtakingly elegant, especially in Cheney (2005), I see a problem in his use of Goodman as "a place on our side of the river to begin building the bridge" from the Western tradition to Native ceremonial worlds (Cheney & Hester 2000: 77). Unfortunately, Goodman *as we find him* cannot span the river, for we will see that his criteria for the *ultimate acceptability* of a world version excludes non-Western versions—including the kind of Native ceremonial worlds Professor Cheney develops. See also Hester and Cheney (2001).

3. See for example Dale Turner (2006) and Russell (2004).

4. This argument was voiced during a session, sponsored by the American Indian Philosophical Association, at the American Philosophical Association Pacific Division meetings in Albuquerque, NM, in March 2000.

5. The "Indian Problem" is, of course, that there are Indians.

6. Recognizing the inherent difficulties in trusting the interpreted narrative *Black Elk Speaks*, I am nonetheless heartened by Deloria's remarks prefacing that narrative: "Present debates center on the question of Neihardt's literary intrusions into Black Elk's system of beliefs and some scholars have said that the book reflects more of Neihardt than it does of Black Elk. It is, admittedly, difficult to discover if we are talking with Black Elk or John Neihardt, whether the vision is to be interpreted

differently, and whether or not the positive emphasis which the book projects is not
the optimism of two poets lost in the modern world and transforming the drabness
into an idealized world. Can it matter? The very nature of great religious teachings
is that they encompass everyone who understands them and personalities become
indistinguishable from the transcendent truth that is expressed. So let it be with
Black Elk Speaks" (Deloria 2000: xvi).

7. I owe much of what I know about the Shawnee language to tribal elder
Rick Nightwolf Wagar, and I thank him here.

8. It is interesting to notice that although European languages have gendered
third-person singular pronouns and possessives, Shawnee has only "willa," which
functions as either "he" or "she" depending on context. But it would be as daft to
suggest that the Shawnee do not recognize gender distinctions as to suggest that
English speakers do not recognize the difference between animate and inanimate
beings. The point is that the more fundamental distinctions will be the ones encoded
grammatically.

Shawnee Thomas Wildcat Alford (1936) makes a similar point when explaining why the Shawnee use the pronoun "he" when speaking of Great Spirit, the
Grandmother: "The pronoun *he* is used in speaking of the Great Spirit because there
is no feminine gender in the Shawnee language. Men and women are spoken of as
of the same gender, only the name of the individual contains the discrimination.
Personal pronouns are neither masculine nor feminine, and most of them are mere
affixes to other words" (19).

9. This is also consistent with Powell's (1877) observation that in American
Indian cosmology "[t]he sun and moon are always personages" (7). Hallowell (1960)
observes a similar notion amongst traditional Ojibwa speakers with respect to the
sun, the "day luminary." In fact, the sun is not only animate, but it is regarded as
an other-than-human person (28–29).

10. At a session on American Indian philosophy at the 2009 American
Philosophical Association Central Division meetings, I asked audience members to
construct the lists. Choctaw Lee Hester included "trees" on his list of persons.

11. Benjamin Franklin quips, "Dost thou love life? Then do not squander
time; for that's the stuff life is made of" ("Benjamin Franklin" 2005), and Calvin
Martin (1999) eloquently and poignantly observes that "[t]ime is the arrow that
wounds me, as I watch myself age and decay and know that time's imperious message is never-ending loss" (7).

2. Nelson Goodman's Constructivism

1. Here's the Berkeleyan challenge: If you believe unperceived material
substance exists, then imagine it—imagine something like your car parked out in
the lot with no one around to perceive it. Oops—you are perceiving it with your
imagining mind! So, unperceived material substance is inconceivable, hence a logical
contradiction, hence metaphysically impossible.

2. An example is the time in chemistry class years ago when at time t_1 I
mixed a little stock hydrochloric acid with zinc metal and at time t_2 I had zinc

chloride and an overabundance of hydrogen gas—and at t_3 there was a note home to my parents; it made a dandy zinc-hydrochloric acid cannon.

3. "Grue" as presently defined is not to be confused with Goodman's "grue," which is defined in the following way: "grue" applies to all things examined before time t just in case they are green but to other things just in case they are blue.

4. That some American Indian languages use what would be understood by an English speaker to be the disjunctive predicate "either blue or green" was understood by Powell (1877) to be a sign that Indians are in the stage of "savagery": "and more: blue and green are not differentiated, for the Indian sees but one color, and has but one name; the green grass and the blue heavens are of the same hue to the Indian eye" (4).

5. Hilary Putnam (1979, 1980, 1981) makes a compelling case for the view he calls *internal realism*. I argued against his internal realism in Norton-Smith (1985), but I have since changed my mind.

I have always found Putnam's second line of argument designed to show the absurdity of metaphysical realism (the alternative to ontological relativity) to be a bit more problematic. According to Putnam, metaphysical realism is the view that (1) there is a world of entities independent of any particular representation, model, theory, or version we have of it, and (2) there is a determinant reference relation between the terms of an intended representation, model, theory, or version of the world and the entities to which the terms refer (Putnam 1979: 125).

Now, Putnam argues that a metaphysical realist who embraces all of the model-theoretic results of classical two-valued semantics, but does not believe in mysterious mental powers, is forced to hold that the reference relation between terms of an intended model and bits of the model-independent world are both fixed and not fixed—a contradiction. For, as a consequence of the Lowenheim-Skolem Theorem, the intended interpretation of a first-order formal system is not fixed by the axioms of the system; indeed, the theorem even implies the existence of non-standard interpretations for first-order number theory. So, the intended interpretation of a first-order system must be fixed by a naturalistic epistemic process, which, in Putnam's view, is knowing the way a language is used. But this "knowing the way a language is used"—specified by meta-linguistic theoretical and operational constraints on language use—is itself expressible in a first-order formal system, and so by Lowenheim-Skolem cannot, in turn, fix the intended interpretation. So, the metaphysical realist who denies mysterious mental processes cannot account for how the intended interpretation is fixed; it is both fixed and not fixed (Norton-Smith 1985).

I do not have much to say about the questions raised by this argument against metaphysical realism, especially because I am now sympathetic to the positive constructivist case. However, I speak on behalf of my friends who are metaphysical realists, for I was one in a past life. First, Putnam believes that scientific theories, belief systems, and theories of language use can be formalized in first-order system. However, it is not universally agreed that our natural language use to express scientific theories or belief systems admits of a first-order formalization. And even if we grant that our natural language could be so formalized, I doubt that the meta-language expressing theoretical and operational constraints of "the total use of language" will be, for it will quantify over the extensions of predicates (or properties), so is best construed as a second-order system. And, there is no second-order analogue to the Lowenheim-Skolem Theorem (Norton-Smith 1985).

6. Goodman's (1977) far more elegant illustration is found in section [I,3] of his *The Structure of Appearance*.

7. By the way, have you ever dropped a feather and a rock? Which falls faster? Was Aristotle wrong? Or, was a methodological assumption made within Galileo's frame of reference to ignore such evidence in favor of an ideal, frictionless physical world?

8. George Berkeley makes a similar point in his critique of John Locke's proposal that we come to have general ideas like whiteness, man, or triangle through a mental process called abstraction. This is supposed to be the process of forming a general idea by focusing on one particular feature of a perceptual experience to the exclusion of all others. So, according to Locke, you can come to have the general idea of whiteness by attending to that feature of the visual experience of the page before you and ignoring the size, shape, texture, and all of its other features. Once armed with the general idea, we can apply it to other perceptual experiences having white among their features.

The problem is that on inspection Berkeley (1982) couldn't find such a general idea as whiteness devoid of all other features. All he could find were particular ideas like the visual experience you are having right now and mental images that are their copies, where whiteness is a property, but so are size and shape. Why believe, then, that we have general ideas like man—which border on the contradictory—because they apply to all particular men, be they tall or small, thin or chubby, hairy or bald, white, black, or copper? *Language* fools us into believing that there is the abstract general idea of whiteness annexed to the word "white." "We have, I think, shown the impossibility of abstract ideas . . . we have traced them to the source from whence they flow, which appears to be language. It cannot be denied that words of are of excellent use, in that by their means all that stock of knowledge that has been purchased by the joint labors of inquisitive men in all ages and nations, may be drawn into the view and made the possession of one single person. But at the same time it must be owned that most parts of knowledge have been strangely perplexed and darkened by the abuse of words, and general ways of speech wherein they are delivered" (19). So beware the "abuse" of language. For a further discussion see Norton-Smith (2001).

9. No doubt that's why I earned a "C–" on the chemistry lab experiment when I found Avagadro's number to be (shockingly) off by a magnitude of 102; my discovery, however, was not telling against the entrenched belief that a mole of a substance contains 6.023×1023 particles.

3. True Versions and Cultural Bias

1. We can establish this, I think, using a nonfallacious analogue to the argument from design. Symbol systems are human constructions (i.e., human products) and so like all other human products must be brought about by human activity.

2. I made some ontological claims in Norton-Smith (1991) I may not now embrace, specifically that there must be unexemplified collective kinds to account for

all of the truths of arithmetic. If not, in the system I proposed then, the statement "Every number has a successor" would be false.

3. A. Irving Hallowell (1960) makes a related observation in his consideration of an Ojibwa worldview. In an animate world brimming with human and other-than-human persons, what a westerner takes to be a regularity based on a causal connection is for an Ojibwa only as reliable as the behavior of a person with identity, autonomy, and volition (29).

4. Vine Deloria (1999) describes other sorts of relationships between persons of various sorts in his essay "Relativity, Relatedness, and Reality" in *Spirit and Reason*. He recounts a story, credited to Standing Bear, demonstrating a plant–human relationship. Then he tells a story about how the "duck brought many good plants and roots to the tribe," evidencing a bird–human relationship. Finally, Deloria describes a buffalo-sunflower relationship—illustrating an animal–plant nexus (34–38).

With all respect to elder Deloria, this points up a fundamental difference between his view of the relationship between the Western world and my own. Deloria's (1999) impressive collection of writings makes clear that he is a *realist*, believing that there is a way the world is apart from human constructive activity. So, he reflects in his essay, "If You Think About It, You Will See That It Is True," that Western science—with a strictly objective, exclusive methodology—arrives at the same sorts of conclusions about the world as a Native subjective, inclusive methodology. Indeed, he even counsels the next generation of American Indians to ground itself in traditional Native knowledge and methodology so that it can contribute to Western science's understanding of the world.

I cannot agree. It seems to me that Deloria's principled position that Native conceptions of knowledge and the natural world can contribute to—even set aright—Western science depends on a pretty liberal interpretation of the kinds and causes of the relativity one finds in each tradition—an interpretation that finds them closely related. However, they are not. The sorts of relativity one finds in the Western Einsteinian world version are neither the same as one finds in the Native world version, nor are they caused by an interconnected nexus of living entities in a living universe. The problem is that in a realist view where the world of facts is the final arbiter of truth, either the Western or Native views—or both—must be false; either the world is living or it is not.

Instead, I must embrace a view that finds the truth in both traditions, that makes truth and knowledge a function of how each tradition categorizes, organizes, and structures the world through symbol systems. Patterns and connections—like the ones Deloria "discovers" between humans, plants, ducks, buffalo, and sunflowers—are "where you find them," that is, constructions in a world version. The same observation holds for the connections "discovered" in Western science.

5. Various versions of "How Buzzard Got His Clothing" abound. See, for example Stonee ("How Buzzard" 1996) and Bruchac (1985).

4. Relatedness, Native Knowledge, and Ultimate Acceptability

1. This, I grant, is circular: "Knowledge is justified by warranting processes." However, in my view the most pressing problem in contemporary Western philosophy

is that of fleshing out the justification clause of the justified true belief analysis of knowledge. I've got my own ideas expressed most recently in Norton-Smith (2004), but this is not my present concern.

2. I owe this interpretation of the story to a comment made by Brian Burkhart in another context during a panel discussion at the 2006 American Philosophical Association Pacific Division meetings. I have made similar observation in the current debate over the use of American Indian imagery. See Norton-Smith (2003).

3. I am well aware, by the way, that authoring this interpretation of American Indian philosophy is no less normative than the actions of our curious Indian and stem cell researcher, and so has moral implications and consequences.

4. Indeed, I argue in Norton-Smith (2004) that an analysis of Shawnee and Ojibwa numerical language indicates an ontological commitment to numerical properties—properties of collections of things grounded in concrete experience—but not to numbers as abstract objects, so a question about the existence of a greatest prime number could not even be meaningfully formulated.

5. Kristine Kurian's observation that true performances are respectfully successful in achieving a goal is closely akin to—if not identical to—Hester and Cheney's (2001) proposal that ceremonial worlds are built around the notion of *responsible truth*:

> a ceremonial world (in the fullest sense of the term) is an actively constructed portrait of the world intended to be responsibly true, one which rings true for everybody's well-being. It is a world built on the basis of an ethical-epistemological orientation of attentiveness (or, as Native Americans tend to put it, *respect*) rather than an epistemology of control. Such ceremonial worlds, built, as they are, around the notion of responsible truth, are not developed piecemeal, but are synthetic creations, adjusted holistically to all the concerns that arise from a focus on responsible truth: they must tie down to the world of everyday practice and experience in a way that makes it possible to survive; they must orient the community and its individuals on roads of life that allow for the flourishing of all members of the community as far as that is possible. (320).

6. It is not surprising, by the way, that Black Hoof's telling should be so close to Tenskwatawa's in many respects, especially the early times, but then differ in how to make sense of their respective circumstances with respect to whites and Christianity. Tecumthe and Tenskwatawa had moved to the Indiana Territory over two decades earlier, resisting American domination, while Black Hoof acquiesced.

7. Indeed, recall that Descartes, the founder of modern Western epistemology, appealed to dreaming as the quintessential nonjustifying experience: How can I know that the visual experience I'm having right now is of my hand, when I've had the same kinds of visual experiences in vivid dreams, but there was no hand before me?

8. The loss of many elders is just one of the many tragedies visited on Native people, especially during the removal. The Cherokee removal during the

harsh winter of 1838–1839 provides a sad example. Four thousand people died in incarceration in stockades before the trek west and during the "Trail of Tears." Of course, the most vulnerable were the first to perish during the forced trek west—the elders. Unlike "literate" traditions, which have access to their entire history, philosophy, literature, and values, oral traditions rely on the elders as the repositories for tribal knowledge, history, and values. In losing the elders, tribes lost their oracles, sages, and libraries.

   9. Gilmore (1919) observes that although Native thought is "at times pitifully infantile . . . reason is on the throne" (8.)

5. An Expansive Conception of Persons

   1. Paul Radin (1972) conveys that the Trickster is "[a]t one and the same time creator and destroyer, giver and negator, he who dupes and who is always duped himself. He wills nothing consciously. At all times he is constrained to behave as he does from impulses over which he has no control" (xxiii). Erdoes and Ortiz (1998) offer a collection of American Indian Trickster tales.

   2. A second misconception, worthy of note but not really worthy of consideration in our main discussion, is that powerful spirit persons are *animals* worshiped by American Indian people. Our "authority" on the subject, Powell (1877), lays out the argument:

> It must be understood that these [gods] have animal forms, but have the power of transforming themselves and assuming any shape at will, anthropomorphic of zoomorphic. This is true also of the beast gods. They can transform themselves, and many wonderful stories are told in their mythology of such transformations. Their hero gods also have the power of transformation, and may be anthropomorphic or zoomorphic. So their . . . gods are animals. (10–11)

The argument is, then, that because Native powerful spirit persons can transform into animal form, they are animals. Similarly, we can argue that because liquid water can transform into ice, liquid water *is* ice. Anyway, based on the same evidence that powerful spirit persons can change into anthropomorphic form, Powell should be able to conclude, "Indian gods are humans." Enough said.

   3. The distinction we are drawing here between human beings and human persons is similar if not identical to one that Viola Cordova (2004) draws in discussing what she calls the Native American ethical system:

> Each new human being born into a group represents an unknown factor to that group. The newborn does not come fully equipped to deal with his membership in the group; he must be taught what it is to be a *human* being in a very specific group. . . . The newborn is at first merely *humanoid*—the group will give him an identity according to their definition of what it is to be human. The primary lesson that is

taught is that the individual's actions have consequences for himself, for others, for the world. The newcomer's *humanness* is measured according to how he comes to recognize that his actions have consequences for others, for the world. (177–78)

The newborn "humanoid" in Cordova's account is a "human being" in ours—an animate being. However, the moral entity Cordova calls a "human being"—an animate being that has internalized the moral lessons of a group—we call a "human person."

    4. Various Algonquin languages have different grammatical constructions for plurals. I use the Shawnee suffix "-ki" for the plural of animate nouns: "manitouki."

    5. I would also venture that despite the philosophical hand-wringing over how knowledge is justified, my colleagues in the Western philosophical tradition know this as well. I really don't want to wrangle with David Hume over whether or not I can experience my mind, or just sensations and perceptions. It doesn't matter.

    6. Deloria (1994) reminds us that behind human kinship with animals and plants is the conception that "they are 'people' in the same manner as the various tribes of human beings are people" (89–90).

    7. I once asked a tribal elder about gifting, and he conveyed that he had "even had some wise old elders tell me that giving is really very selfish because of the mechanism of how the Universe works." We are all related and in giving one is ensuring that one receives in return.

6. The Semantic Potency of Performance

    1. Although sorting and collecting are different kinds of activities, my constructive realism regards both as the realistically construed kinds of world-constructing activities that are logically prior to any world version whatsoever. Kris Kurian suggests that *greetings* are a way of categorizing the world into acquaintances and nonacquaintances. She also makes the interesting claim that *marking time*—a wide range of performances that organize and are organized by the temporal—creates worlds. (By the way, we're in the midst of a monster March 2008 snowstorm in Ohio, and while shoveling the 18 inches of snow off my driveway it occurred to me that *shoveling* is also a performance that reorganizes the world.)

    2. Gill uses the somewhat unfortunate term *nonliterate*—with many well-intended qualifications. However, although Gill's sense of *nonliterate* is neither "illiterate," "preliterate" nor "stupid," it carries such negative connotations. So, I avoid it.

    3. According to Cheney and Hester (2000), "The performative dimension of language should be understood as fundamental—not just in obviously religious settings, but *generally*. . . . We *do* things with words. Foremost among these performative functions is the creation of what I call the ceremonial worlds in which we live. Other performative functions of language are possible only within these *ceremonial*

worlds—promise making, for instance, is possible only within an accepted set of social conventions, as is the progress achieved within science" (79–80).

4. And may I take this opportunity to point out to my Turtle brothers that the Turkey is by far the best *um'soma*.

5. The "tribes" extant at the time of the Trowbridge (1939) interview were snake, turtle, raccoon, turkey, hawk, deer, bear, wolf, panther, elk, buffalo, and tree.

6. The full text of William Penn's letter appears in Mombert (1869). See Google Book Search (2008) http://books.google.com/books?id=PMBEP_WoeIQC.

7. In 1690, when Locke published his *Second Treatise*, Europeans already had been in the Americas for almost 200 years. Beaver skins had become the first cash crop of North America and as a result of trade with the French, and later the British and the Dutch, the Iroquois had trapped out the beaver in their home lands by the 1640s. This precipitated the "Beaver Wars" in the latter half of the seventeenth century, as the Iroquois aggressively expanded towards the Ohio country (Hurt 1998). The Shawnee located in Pennsylvania, West Virginia, and Kentucky respond by splitting into a number of groups based on their five traditional divisions and moving off in various directions (Howard 1981). Marquette describes Shawnee villages in the Ohio Valley in 1673 (Calloway 1995: 160). In about 1690, a great Shawnee eastern migration occurred; they joined Delaware villages along the lower Susquehanna in eastern Pennsylvania (Calloway 1995; Galloway 1934).

8. Unfortunately, in making his case against Lockean liberalism and in developing his own influential account of gifting traditions, Mauss embraces the assumption that such "archaic" societies, "societies that we lump together somewhat awkwardly as primitive or inferior . . . have precede our own" (5). That is, Mauss apparently accepts the same assumption that societies evolve over time from the primitive to the civilized as Powell.

9. Seth Mallios (2006) penned an excellent analysis of the variable and confusing relationships between colonists at Ajacan, Roanoke, and Jamestown and the Chesapeake Algonquins. Mallios argues that these relationships began amicably, but soon turned antagonistic because the Europeans regarded exchange as barter, whereas the Algonquins viewed exchange as gifting. So, from the Native perspective, a gift inadequately reciprocated—or not reciprocated at all—was an affront to be justly answered with violence.

10. Although we earlier observed that a tradition's conception of human beings and their relationships with other entities in the nonhuman world influences the nature of each kind of exchange; gifting in Native traditions is quite unlike gifting in the Western tradition.

11. This should seem entirely reasonable to anyone who cares for a family heirloom; I am obligated to keep my grandmother's old Sellars hoosier, gifted to me after she passed.

12. Dr. Mayer made this comment during a consideration of her book, *Cries from a Metis Heart*, at a session of the American Philosophical Association Pacific Division meetings in Pasadena, March 22, 2008.

Cheney and Hester (2000) characterize *respect* in indigenous ceremonial worlds as a "thick epistemological concept," as "a particular way of being aware in the world" (82):

Imagine a deep practice of universal consideration for all beings (including what Euro-Americans would call "things"), a consideration, a considerateness, that is not instituted as a moral principle or rule governing behavior, but is a dimension of one's very *perception* in the world. Such a conception is present in the notion of "respect" for all beings that is pervasive in indigenous cultures. (81).

In Hester and Cheney (2001), *respect* is characterized more appropriately, I think, as an "ethical-epistemological orientation of attentiveness," although I, throughout my exploration, emphasize the normative dimensions of respect.

7. Circularity as a World-Ordering Principle

1. We may observe, again, the genesis of the idea that American Indians understood the sacred in spatial and not temporal terms in the remarks of Powell (1877):

A savage philosopher believes in a system of worlds, not globes swinging in the heavens, but places of existence—the world of this life, the land on which we tread and the water in which we swim—and the world or worlds of land and water to which we go. Among the different tribes of North America, two methods in the arrangement of worlds are observed. The lower tribes have their worlds arranged horizontally or topographically; the Nu-gun-tu-wip, the ghost land, the land of the hereafter, is beyond some great topographical feature. . . . The coast tribes say "beyond the sea;" the dweller on the river banks, "beyond the river;" tribes who dwell in valleys surrounded by crags and peaks say, "beyond the mountains;" the tribes who dwell on the brinks of the great canons, "beyond the chasm." Among those tribes having their worlds arranged topographically, a past world is not an item in their philosophy. (6)

2. Thanks to Kris Kurian and Carli Waller.
3. The sense of "abstract" in Fixico's observation about the transmission of knowledge in American Indian traditions is, I think, "perplexing or obscure for the Western linear mind," because the observation is often made that the Native turn of mind is nonlinear and closely tied to experience; indeed, I argued in Norton-Smith (2004) that the traditional Algonquin conception of the numbers is *not* that they are objects with an *abstract* existence, but that numbers are conceived of nominalistically as properties of collections of things or events, whether concrete or not. The Indian nonlinear mind, as well as the Western perplexity with (and intolerance) of it, is nicely captured by Beverly Slapin's (2006) "Two Plus Two or Why Indians Flunk":

All right, class, let's see who knows what two plus two is. Yes, Doris?

I have a question. Two plus two what?

Two plus two anything.

I don't understand.

OK, Doris, I'll explain it to you. You have two apples and you get two more. How many do you have?

Where would I get two more?

From a tree.

Why would I pick two apples if I already have two?

Never mind, you have two apples and someone gives you two more.

Why would someone give me two more, if she could give them to someone who's hungry?

Doris, it's just an example.

An example of what?

Let's try again—you have two apples and you find two more. Now how many do you have?

Who lost them?

YOU HAVE TWO PLUS TWO APPLES!!!! HOW MANY DO YOU HAVE ALL TOGETHER????

Well, if I ate one, and gave away the other three, I'd have none left, but I could always get some more if I got hungry from that tree you were talking about before.

Doris, this is your last chance—you have two, uh, buffalo, and you get two more. Now how many do you have?

It depends. How many are cows and how many are bulls, and is any of the cows pregnant?

It's hopeless! You Indians have absolutely no grasp of abstractions!

Huh? (21. Used with permission of the author)

4. We do not know what the Hopewell called themselves. The name "Hopewell" comes from Capt. M. C. Hopewell, on whose property the Hopewell Earthworks were located (Romain 2000).

Some may object to an appeal to the Middle Woodland Hopewell—a "pre-historic" people (by Western lights)—in order to evidence circularity as an ordering principle in more recent "historic" American Indian world versions. But then I am reminded of all of the elements of Platonism still evident in contemporary Western thought—and not just embraced by the philosophical elite—for neo-Platonism's influence on everyday Christianity is very well known. Despite the obvious differences between Western and indigenous traditions in content and transmission, it is neither impossible nor implausible that ways of ordering the world that are at the core of the Hopewell world version are still extant in more recent Native versions.

Bibliography

Adams, Douglas. *The More Than Complete Hitchhiker's Guide*. Stamford, CT: Longmeadow Press, 1987.

Alford, Thomas Wildcat. *Civilization (As Told To Florence Drake)*. Norman: University of Oklahoma Press, 1936.

"Benjamin Franklin." *Quote DB*. 2005. 3 January 2008 <http://www.quotedb.com/quotes/460>.

Beck, David R. M. "The Myth of the Vanishing Race." *Edward S. Curtis and The North American Indian*. Northwestern University and American Memory Project, Library of Congress., 2001.http://memory.loc.gov/ ammem/award98/ ienhtml/essay2.html (accessed January 3, 2008).

Berkeley, George. *A Treatise Concerning the Principles of Human Knowledge*. Indianapolis: Hackett Publishing Company, 1982.

Black Elk, Nicholas, and John Neihardt. *Black Elk Speaks*. Lincoln: University of Nebraska Press, 2000.

Bruchac, Joseph. *Iroquois Stories: Heroes and Heroines, Monsters and Magic*. Trumansburg, NY: The Crossing Press, 1985.

Burkhart, Brian Yazze. "What Coyote and Thales Can Teach Us: An Outline of American Indian Epistemology." In Waters, *American Indian Thought*, 15–26.

Byers, A. M. "Social Structure and the Pragmatic Meaning of Material Culture." In Pacheco, *A View From the Core*, 176–192.

Cajete, George. "Philosophy of Native Science." In Waters, *American Indian Thought*, 45–57.

Callicot, J. Baird. *In Defense of the Land Ethic*. Albany: State University of New York Press, 1989.

Calloway, Colin G. *The American Revolution in Indian Country*. Cambridge: Cambridge University Press, 1995.

Cartwright, Nancy. *How the Laws of Physics Lie*. Oxford: Oxford University Press, 1983.

Cheney, Jim. "Truth, Knowledge and the Wild World." *Ethics & the Environment* 10, no. 2 (2005): 101–135.

——— and Lee Hester. "Ceremonial Worlds and Environmental Sanity." *Strategies: Journal of Theory, Culture and Politics* 13, no. 1 (2000): 77–87.

Closs, Michael P. *Native American Mathematics*. Austin: University of Texas Press, 1986.

153

Cordova, Viola. "Ethics: The We and the I. "In Waters, *American Indian Thought*, 173–181.

Cowan, C. W. "Social Implications of Ohio Hopewell Art." In Pacheco, *A View From the Core*,130–148.

Dabe, Bryan. "The Shawnee." Unpublished manuscript, 1994.

Deloria, Jr., Vine. "Foreword." In *Black Elk Speaks*, by Nicholas Black Elk and John Neihardt, xiii–xvii. Lincoln: University of Nebraska Press, 2000.

———. *God is Red: A Native View of Religion*. Golden, CO: Fulcrum Publishing, 1994.

———. "Philosophy and Tribal Peoples." In Waters, *American Indian Thought*, 3–11.

———. *Spirit and Reason*. Eds. B. Deloria, K. Foehner and S. Scinta. Golden, CO: Fulcrum Publishing, 1999.

Dennett, Daniel. *Brainstorms*. Montgomery, VT: Bradford Books, 1978.

———. "Conditions of Personhood." In *The Identity of Persons*, edited by A. Rorty, 175–96. Berkeley: University of California Press, 1976.

Denny, J. Peter. "Cultural Ecology of Mathematics: Ojibway and Inuit Hunters." In Closs, *Native American Mathematics*, 129–80.

Descartes, René. *Meditations on First Philosophy*. 3rd ed. Translated by Donald Cress. Indianapolis: Hackett, 1993.

Eckert, Allan W. *The Conquerors*. Ashland, KY: Jesse Stuart Foundation, 2002.

Erdoes, Richard, and Alfaonso Ortiz, eds. *American Indian Myths and Legends*. New York: Pantheon Books, 1984.

———, eds. *American Indian Trickster Tales*. London: Penguin, 1998.

Fitzgerald, Michael O., ed. *The Essential Charles Eastman*. Bloomington, IN: World Wisdom, Inc, 2007.

Fixico, Donald. *The American Indian Mind in a Linear World*. New York: Routledge, 2003.

Frankfurt, H. "Freedom of the Will and the Concept of a Person." *The Journal of Philosophy* 68 (1971): 5–20.

Galloway, W. A. *Old Chillicothe: Shawnee and Pioneer History, Conflicts and Romances in the Northwest Territory*. Xenia, OH: The Buckeye Press, 1934.

Gill, Sam D. "Holy Book in Nonliterate Traditions: Toward the Reinvention of Religion." In *Native American Religious Action: A Performance Approach to Religion*, edited by Sam D. Gill 129–46. Columbia: University of South Carolina Press, 1987.

———. *Native American Religions*. Belmont, CA: Wadsworth Publishing Co., 1982.

Gilmore, G. W. *Animism or Thought Currents of Primitive Peoples*. Boston: Marshall Jones Company, 1919. *Sacred-texts.com*. September 2000. May 15, 2008 <http://www.sacred-texts.com/sha/anim>.

Godelier, Maurice. *The Enigma of the Gift*. Chicago: University of Chicago Press, 1999.

Goodman, Nelson. *Fact, Fiction, and Forecast*. Cambridge, MA: Harvard University Press, 1983.

———. *Of Minds and Other Matters*. Cambridge, MA: Harvard University Press, 1984.

———. *Problems and Projects*. Indianapolis, IN: Bobbs-Merrill, 1972.

———. *The Structure of Appearance*. Dordrecht, Holland: D. Reidel, 1977.

———. *Ways of Worldmaking*. 1978. Indianapolis, IN: Hackett, 1988.

Goodman, Nelson, and Cathrine Elgin. *Reconceptions in Philosophy and Other Arts and Sciences*. Indianapolis, IN: Hackett, 1988.

Hallowell, A. Irving. "Ojibwa Ontology, Behavior, and World View." In *Culture in History: Essays in Honor of Paul Radin*, edited by S. Diamond, 19–52. New York: Columbia University Press, 1960.

Hanke, Lewis. *Aristotle and the American Indians*. London: Hollis & Carter, 1959.

Harvey, Henry. *History of the Shawnee Indians (from the Year 1681 to 1854 inclusive)*. Cincinnati, OH: Ephraim Morgan & Sons, 1855.

Hester, Lee, and Jim Cheney. "Truth and Native American Epistemology." *Social Epistemology* 15, no.4 (2001): 319–34.

Hively, Ray, and Robert Horn. "Geometry and Astronomy in Prehistoric Ohio." *Journal for the History of Astronomy* 13, no. 4 (1982): S1–S20.

———. "A Statistical Study of Lunar Alignments at the Newark Earthworks." *Midcontinental Journal of Archaeology* 31, no. 2 (2006). FindArticles.com. http://findarticles.com/p/articles/mi_qa3904/is_200610/ai_n17196910/. (accessed August 29, 2009)

Hobhouse, L. T. *Morals in Evolution*. New York: Henry Holt Co., 1907.

"How Buzzard Got His Clothing." *Stonee's Lore, Legends and Teachings*. 1996. StoneE Producktions. http://www.ilhawaii.net/~stony/ 1296myth.html (accessed February 25, 2009).

Howard, James. *Shawnee! The Ceremonialism of a Native Indian Tribe and Its Cultural Background*. Athens: Ohio University Press, 1981.

Hurt, R. D. *The Ohio Frontier: Crucible of the Old Northwest, 1720–1830*. Bloomington: Indiana University Press, 1998.

Jojola, Ted. "Notes on Identity, Time, Space, and Place." In Waters, *American Indian Thought*, 87–96.

Jones, W. "The Algonkin Manitu." *Journal of American Folklore* 18 (1905): 183–90.

Kant, Immanuel. *Groundwork of the Metaphysic of Morals*. Translated by H. J. Paton. New York: Harper & Row, 1964.

Keeshig-Tobias, Lenore. "Those Anthropologists." In Slapin and Seale, *Through Indian Eyes*, 42.

Kinietz, Vernon, and Ermine W. Voegelin, eds. *Shawnese Traditions: C. C. Trowbridge's Account*. Ann Arbor: University of Michigan Press, 1939.

Kitcher, Philip. *The Nature of Mathematical Knowledge*. Oxford: Oxford University Press, 1984.

Knapp, Joseph. Newark Works, Licking County Ohio by Whittlesey, Squire and Davis." *Copperas*. August 21, 1998. http://coolohio.com/octagon/Nwk_wrks.gif (accessed April 28, 2008).

Kurian, Kristine. "A Discussion on True Goals and Processes." Unpublished manuscript, 2008.

Leading Cloud, Jenny. "Coyote, Iktome, and the Rock." In *American Indian Myths and Legends*, edited by Richard Erdoes and Alfonso Ortiz, 337–39. New York: Pantheon Books, 1984.

Lepper, Bradley. "The Newark Earthworks and the Geometric Enclosures of the Scioto Valley: Connections and Conjectures." In Pacheco, *A View From the Core*, 226–41.

Locke, John. *An Essay Concerning Human Understanding*. Edited by P. H. Nidditch. Oxford: Clarendon Press, 1991.

———. *The Second Treatise on Civil Government*. Buffalo, NY: Prometheus, 1986.

Mallios, Seth. *The Deadly Politics of Giving*. Tuscaloosa: University of Alabama Press, 2006.

Martin, Calvin L. *The Way of the Human Being*. New Haven, CT: Yale University Press, 1999.

"The Matrix." Dirs. Wachowski, Andy and Larry Wachowski. With Keanu Reeves, Lawrence Fishburne, Carrie-Anne Moss, Hugo Weaving, and Joe Pantoliano. Warner Bros. and Village Roadshow Pictures, 1999.

Mauss, Marcel. *The Gift: The Form and Reason for Exchange*. Translated by W. D. Hall. New York: W. W. Norton, 2000.

Mayer, Lorraine. *Cries from a Metis Heart*. Winnipeg: Pemmican Publications, 2007.

Mombert, J. E. *An Authentic History of Lancaster County: In the State of Pennsylvania*. Lancaster, PA: J. E. Barr & Co., 1869.

"Moundbuiders County Club." http://www.moundbuilderscc.com/. (accessed August 29, 2009).

Mount, Steve. "Constitutional Topic: Article 1, Section 8." *USConstitution.net*. July 31, 2007. http://www.usconstitution.net/const.html#A1Sec8. (accessed December 6, 2007).

Myers, P., R. Espinosa, C. S. Parr, T. Jones, G. S. Hammond, and T. A. Dewey. 2008. The Animal Diversity Web (online). Accessed August 28, 2009 at http://animaldiversity.org.

NASA. "Speed of the Earth's Rotation." December 1, 2005. http://imagine.gsfc.nasa.gov/docs/ask_astro/answers/970401c.html (accessed May 12, 2007).

Nerlich, Graham. *Values and Valuing: Speculations on the Ethical Life of Persons*. Oxford: Clarendon Press, 1989.

Nietzsche, Friedrich. *Beyond Good and Evil*. Translated by Helen Zimmern. Buffalo, NY: Prometheus, 1989.

Norton-Smith, Thomas M. "An Arithmetic of Actions Kinds: Kitcher Gone Mad(dy)." *Philosophical Studies* 63 (1991): 217–30.

———. "A Consideration of Hilary Putnam." *Auslegung* 11, no. 2 (1985): 493–504.

———. "Indigenous Numerical Thought in Two American Indian Tribes." In Waters, *American Indian Thought*, 58–71.

———. "A Note on Philip Kitcher's Analysis of Mathematical Truth." *Notre Dame Journal of Formal Logic* 33 (1992): 136–39.

———. "Sending an Irishman 'Realing': Constructive Realism and George Berkeley's Philosophy of Arithmetic." *The Midwest Quarterly* 42, no. 2 (2001): 199–211.

———. "What a Puzzle Teaches about Moral Justifications For and Against the Use of American Indian Sports Team Imagery." *Ayaangwaamizin* 3, no. 1 (2003): 19–30.

"person." *Dictionary.com Unabridged (v 1.1)*. 2004. Random House, Inc. Dictionary. com http://dictionary.reference.com/browse/person (accessed January 14, 2008).

Poole, Ross. "On Being a Person." *Australasian Journal of Philosophy* 74, no. 1 (1996): 38–56.

Powell, John W. *Outlines of the Philosophy of the North American Indians*. New York: Douglas Taylor, Book, Job and Law Printer, 1877.

Putnam, Hilary. "Models of Reality." *Journal of Symbolic Logic* 45 no. 3 (1980): 464–82.

———. "Realism and Reason." *Meaning and the Moral Sciences*. London: Routledge & Kegan Paul, 1979. 123–38.

———. *Reason, Truth and History*. Cambridge: Cambridge University Press, 1981.

Quine, W.V.O. *World & Object*. Cambridge, MA: MIT Press, 1960.

Radin, Paul. *The Trickster: A Study in American Indian Mythology*. New York: Schocken Books, 1972.

Ridout, Thomas. *Ridout's Vocabulary of Shawnee*. Merchantville, NJ: Evolution Publishing, 2006.

Romain, W. F. *The Mysteries of the Hopewell*. Akron, OH: University of Akron Press, 2000.

———. "Newark Earthwork Cosmology: This Island Earth." *Hopewell Archeology: The Newsletter of Hopewell Archeology in the Ohio River Valley* 6, no. 2 (2005). http://www.nps.gov/mwac/hopewell/v6n2/one.htm (accessed May 3, 2008).

Russell, Steve. "The Jurisprudence of Colonialism." In Waters, *American Indian Thought*, 217–28.

Sigel, I. E. "Is the Concept of the Concept Still Elusive or What Do We Know About Concept Development?" In *New Trends in Conceptual Representation: Challenges to Piaget?* edited by E. K. Scholnick, 239–74. Hillsdale, NJ: Lawrence Erlbaum Associates, 1983.

Skinner, A. and J. Satterlee. "The Man Who Loved the Frog Songs." *Anthropological Papers of the American Museum of Natural History: Forklore of the Menomini Indians* Vol. XIII, Part III. New York, 1915.

Slapin, Beverly. "Two Plus Two or Why Indians Flunk." *Through Indian Eyes: The Native Experience in Books for Children* Edited by Beverly Slapin, and Doris Seale Berkeley, CA: Oyate Publishing, 2006. 21

Smith, Thomas M. "An Introduction to Intuitionist Mathematics." MS thesis, Pittsburg State University, 1981.

Squier, Ephraim G., and Edwin H. Davis. *Ancient Monuments of the Mississippi Valley*. edited by David J. Meltzer. Washington: Smithsonian Institution Press, 1998.

Standing Bear, Luther. *My Indian Boyhood*. Lincoln: University of Nebraska Press, 2006.

Thom, Dark Rain. *Kohkumthena's Grandchildren: The Shawnee*. Indianapolis: Guild Press of Indiana, 1994.

Trowbridge, Charles C. *Shawnese Traditions*. Edited V. Kinietz and E. Voegelin. Ann Arbor: University of Michigan Press, 1939.

Turner, Dale. *This is Not a Peace Pipe: Towards a Critical Indigenous Philosophy*. Toronto: University of Toronto Press, 2006.

"The Twilight Zone: Time Enough at Last." *TV.com*. 2009. CBS Interactive. http://www.tv.com/the-twilight-zone/time-enough-at-last/episode/   12592/summary.html (accessed March 23, 2009).

Voegelin, C. F. "Shawnee Stems and the Jacob P. Dunn Miami Dictionary." *Indiana Historical Society Prehistory Research Series* 1, no. 8 (1939): 289–341.

———. "Shawnee Stems and the Jacob P. Dunn Miami Dictionary." *Indiana Historical Society Prehistory Research Series* 1, no. 10 (1940): 409–78.

———, and E. W. Voegelin. "Shawnee Name Groups." *American Anthropologist* New Series 37, no. 4 (1935): 617–35.

Waters, Anne., ed. *American Indian Thought*. Oxford: Blackwell Publishing, 2004a.

———. "Language Matters: Nondiscrete Nonbinary Dualism." 2004b. In Waters, *American Indian Thought*, 97–115.

Whitt, Laurie A. "Biocolonialism and the Commodification of Knowledge." In Waters, *American Indian Thought*, 188–213.

"Willem de Vlamingh, Explorer." *VOC Historical Society*. July 23, 2003. http://www.voc.iinet.net.au/vlamingh.html (accessed June 18, 2007).

Wynn, Karen. "Addition and Subtraction by Human Infants." *Nature* 358 (1992a): 749–50.

———. "Children's Acquisition of the Number Words and the Counting System." *Cognitive Psychology* 24 (1992b): 220–51.

———. "Children's Understanding of Number." *Cognition* 36 (1990): 155–193.

Index

linear ordering principle, 119, 122,
    124, 133. *See also* Fixico, Donald, on
    the Western linear mind
Locke, John: abstract ideas, 144n8;
    civil and liberal societies, 106–108,
    110; and gifting, 106, 110–111; and
    Indians, 107, 111, 149n7; and Mauss,
    110–111 (*see* Mauss); persons, 78–81,
    90, 106–107; property and barter,
    106–108, 111
logic, nondiscrete nonbinary, 44–45, 64
logic, intuitionist, 44
Lowenheim-Skolem theorem, 32,
    143n5

Mallios, Seth, 149n9
"The Man Who Loved the Frog
    Songs," 58–59, 100
manitou, 86–91, 93, 148n4. *See also*
    spirit
Maori, 109, 115
Marietta Earthworks, 132. *See also*
    Hopewell
Martin, Calvin, 89, 91, 101, 114, 122,
    142n11
Mauss, Marcel: gifting obligations,
    109, 112–115; critique of Lockean
    liberal political theory, 108, 110–111,
    149n8; critique of utilitarianism, 108,
    112
Mayer, Lorraine, 112, 149n12
McCormick, Bernard, 39
meaning-shaping principle of action, 63
Melanesian peoples, 108
Menominee, 58–59, 100
minds, argument for, 87–88
Moluntha, 67
moral universe, 49, 59, 61, 63–65, 75
Mound City, 132
Muscogee Creek. *See* Creek

naïve realism, 18, 23, 51
NASA, 18, 19, 21, 43, 47
National Congress of American
    Indians, 3

Native knowledge. *See* American
    Indian knowledge
Native world version. *See* American
    Indian world version
nature: American Indian concept, 13,
    47, 49, 50, 84, 120–122, 125, 122,
    125, 137, 142n6; Lockean concept,
    106–107, 108, 110, 111
Navajo. *See* Dine
von Neumann, John, 27, 31
Newark Earthworks, 130–132. *See also*
    Hopewell
Nietzsche, Friedrich, 40
Northwest coast Indians, 78
Norton-Smith, Thomas, xiii, 27–28,
    143n5

Ohiyesa. *See* Eastman, Charles
Ojibwa: dreams, 72; language, 42,
    84, 86, 142n9, 146n4; concept of
    persons, 84, 89, 90, 94, 145n3;
    sacred stories, 100; spirits, 86; stones
    animate, 88–89; worldview, 145n3
ontological pluralism, 26–32, 52
ontological relativity, 27
Open Door. *See* Tenskwatawa
oral traditions, 5, 11–13, 65–68, 97,
    100, 147n8
ordering, 23, 25–26, 39, 40, 43, 51, 58,
    96, 105, 116, 117, 119, 120. *See also*
    world-constructing processes
origin stories, 65–68, 100
Ottawa, 86

Parmenter, Jim, 1
Penn, William, 105, 111
performance: dance, 37, 101–102,
    135, 137; gifting, 93, 99, 105–115,
    109, 112, 114, 137; and knowledge,
    58, 60–63, 74, 97; and moral
    content, 65, 66, 129; ontological
    consequences, 96; semantic potency
    of 1, 3, 11, 14, 95–117, 136–137;
    speech acts, 12, 99–101, 137; as
    story-telling, 66–68, 100–101 (*see*